VICTORIAN FASHIONS AND COSTUMES

FROM HARPER'S BAZAR

1867-1898

OVER 1000 ILLUSTRATIONS

Edited
and with an Introduction by

Stella Blum

DOVER PUBLICATIONS, INC., NEW YORK

Published in Canada by General Publishing Company, Ltd., 30 Lesmill Road, Don Mills, Toronto, Ontario.
Published in the United Kingdom by Constable and Company, Ltd., 10 Orange Street, London WC 2.

Victorian Fashions and Costumes from Harper's Bazar is a new work, first published by Dover Publications in 1974.

DOVER *Pictorial Archive* SERIES

This volume belongs to the Dover Pictorial Archive Series. Up to ten illustrations from this book may be reproduced on any one project or in any single publication, free and without special permission. Wherever possible include a credit line indicating the title of this book, editor and publisher. Please address the publisher for permission to make more extensive use of illustrations than that authorized above.
The republication of this book in whole is prohibited.

International Standard Book Numbers
(Clothbound): 0-486-23083-X
(Paperbound): 0-486-22990-4
Library of Congress Catalog Card Number: 73-92635

Manufactured in the United States of America
Dover Publications, Inc.
180 Varick Street
New York, N.Y. 10014

❧ INTRODUCTION ❧

The Birth of 'Harper's Bazar'

Harper's Bazar was a major American fashion journal from its first publication in 1867 until 1898, when it began to decline in importance, losing its readership to more modern publications such as *Vogue*. (In 1913, *Harper's* regained prestige under the guidance of William Randolph Hearst.) Selections from a complete run of *Harper's* for these years provide a rare opportunity to examine changes in Victorian fashion and taste —hardly perceptible when viewed year by year, yet obvious when seen in broader perspectives.

By 1867, the Civil War concluded, America was settling down into more peaceful pursuits. With growing affluence, more leisure time, and improved communications and travel facilities, America's now sizable upper-middle class grew more sophisticated. It looked to Europe for leadership in fashions and taste. Foreign magazines became more available and some, such as the German *Die Modenwelt*, not only had a number of European editions, but also one in New York, called *The Season*.

The year 1867 also marks the date of the International Exhibition in Paris, which attracted many American businessmen and merchants. The wives and daughters who accompanied them returned with trunks filled with French treasures for their wardrobes. How much they were treasured is attested by the number of well-preserved French-made dresses that have survived to become part of present costume collections.

A few years before the Exhibition, Charles Frederick Worth, an Englishman working in Paris, started the practice of showing completed gowns on live mannequins to prospective customers. The idea proved very successful and led to the establishment of the French couture. By 1867, however, Mr. Worth had become as selective about his clients as he was about his fabrics and trimmings, and it was the dream of every fashion-minded woman both here and abroad to own a gown by Worth; to have one was to be in league with the queens and princesses whom he dressed.

American shops, alert to this Francomania, imported whatever they could—dresses, fabrics, laces and ribbons—in the hope of pleasing those of their clients who could not go to Paris. The ladies themselves sought out clever dressmakers to try to reproduce, as best they could, the gowns shown in French fashion plates.

Although Paris was fashion's focal point, London also claimed its share of attention. In 1860 the Prince of Wales, later Edward VII, decided to visit the United States. The event unleashed rounds of social festivities unlike any before in the history of the country. America dined with him, danced with him and watched his every move, thoroughly enchanted by this heady sampling of royalty. In 1863 Edward married Alexandra, a beautiful Danish princess. Unlike Queen Victoria, who had given herself up entirely to mourning the death of her husband, the Prince and Princess of Wales were gay and socially active people who dressed well and set fashions. Americans, feeling closer to English royalty after the young Prince's visit to their shores, continued to follow the activities of the English court and developments in English fashions—especially sporting fashions—with great interest.

It was into this era that *Harper's Bazar*, "A repository of Fashion, Pleasure and Instruction," made its entrance on November 2, 1867. Published in New York by Harper and Brothers, the magazine came out every Saturday and sold for ten cents a copy or "$4.00 a year in advance." According to its first editorial, its aim was to be a publication which would combine the useful with the beautiful. Although it would include everything that would be interesting to the family circle, it was largely intended for ladies. "In this connection the fashions are naturally an important subject: three hundred millions of dollars being annually expended in this country for dry goods, the making up of which is executed or superintended almost wholly by the female portion of the household."

The editorial also went on to explain that special arrangements had been made with leading European journals, particularly with the German *Der Bazar* whereby *Harper's Bazar* would receive fashion designs in advance and publish them at the same time that they appeared in Paris, Berlin and other European cities. "Our readers will thus be sure of obtaining the genuine Paris fashions simultaneously with Parisians themselves." Fashions in vogue in New York, "which may be styled the Paris of America," would also be featured. Along with this would be combined fancy work of all kinds and useful suggestions for dressmaking, including patterns accompanied by plain and practical directions. The editorial concludes with "a Fervent wish that *Harper's*

Bazar may accomplish at least a part of our desires and contribute to increase the happiness of American families.''

Harper's Bazar was something new, as different from the existing American magazines as it was from the French. The American periodicals—*Godey's Lady's Book, Peterson's Magazine, Frank Leslie's Gazette of Fashion* and a number of lesser-known magazines—devoted most of their pages to utilitarian wear suited to the American way of life as it was then conceived. The fashion plates in these magazines were usually redrawn from French periodicals, and were often printed a year or more after their intitial appearance. The French magazines were quite the opposite of the American publications. They were aloof to the practical aspects of life and showed fashions in delicate, highly idealized color illustrations.

Harper's Bazar had a more solid appearance, with carefully detailed engravings in black and white. Many of the designs included were directly of European origin, but selected with an American audience in mind. Most of the others were based on Eurpean models, but had been altered to meet American tastes and needs. Many were translated into patterns so complicated that only an expert can decipher them today. Some of these patterns were printed in the magazine (Visiting Dress, p. 22 and Trained House Dress, p. 26); additional ones could be purchased from the publisher.

Fashion, 1867–1898; Trends and Practices

Fashions are as complex as the people who create and accept them, and represent biological and environmental forces acting on individuals. The intent of this book, however, is not to examine the deeper implications, although they do exist, but to act as a survey of fashions as they were recorded in *Harper's Bazar* from 1867 to 1898. The plates were chosen not only to show changing cycles of dress, but also the rich variations within the cycles. Consideration was also given to fashions that reflected the manners, customs and habits of Americans in the upper-middle class.

Fashion entails constant change, but the manner in which it changes varies according to a general pattern. At first a new silhouette is quickly evolved. During its evolution, it is worn simply, with little trimming. Once the form has established itself, the development of the silhouette slows down, and the process of decoration begins to build up a fresh aspect to the fashion. Then the silhouette changes again. In the period 1867–98, styles for women evolved rather steadily according to this pattern, the forms changing in cycles of approximately eight years' duration each. This book divides the major fashion configurations or ''looks'' of the late nineteenth century into four sections: 1867–74, Bustles and Puffs; 1875–82, Natural Form and Cuirass Body; 1883–90, Return of the Bustle; 1891–98, Hourglass Figure. This is not to say that the gowns of 1874 were totally different from those of 1875, or that there was an abrupt change of fashion in 1883. On the whole fashions are of an evolutionary rather than revolutionary nature. Old styles merge with new, as in Ladies' Spring and Summer Wrappings, 1869, and Ladies' and Children's Walking, House, and Evening Dresses, 1870, where one finds gowns with the earlier long straight trained skirts along with the newer draped up ones (pp. 14–15, 28–29). By the same token, the seeds of the next cycle begin to appear within a current cycle. Figure b, Evening and Street Dresses, 1881, shows a gown with the sides of the skirt pulled back ''à la polonaise,'' (p. 133). This bunching at the sides and the back eventually grows into the huge bustles of the mid-1880s. Sometimes elements of a fashion are retained and are merely altered to conform to new silhouettes. The Cuirass Basque, 1875, Single-breasted Square Coat, 1876, and Fur and Fur Trimming, 1885, illustrate various versions of a similar back (pp. 80, 107, 187). Although there is a definite resemblance in the treatment, they are years apart and well within their contemporary mold.

Unlike the present, when it is possible for a woman to wear one costume all day and, with only a change of accessories, to appear fashionably dressed for a full schedule of activities, in the nineteenth century a lady had to furnish her wardrobe with a great variety of costumes. She would need gowns for the morning hours, for afternoons at home, for visiting, for dinners, or for receptions and balls. Periods of mourning were long and called for rigid observance (Mourning Attire, p. 291). Naturally, weddings and honeymoons were great occasions to be marked with sumptuous bridal gowns, going-away costumes and second-day dresses. Communions and Confirmations also called for special dress (Confirmation Dress, pp. 52, 120). There were costumes for promenading and costumes for traveling. A rather splendid wardrobe was required at summer resorts. ''For a summer's sojourn at a fashionable waterplace an outfit as complete as a trousseau is required, and the whole world of costly fabrics may be employed in creating it.''

The races called for an elaborate day dressing since the ladies used the track as a place to exhibit their clothes and set fashions. Just how important the racetrack was as a showcase can be seen in an article in which there was a discussion as to whether the ''tournure'' or bustle was to continue to be worn or not. ''The Grand Prix decided the question. Stuart was not the only victor on that occasion. The tournure too, came ahead'' (July 28, 1888).

Although for their day and evening fashions the Americans looked to Paris for direction, they borrowed from the English for sports and the costumes for them. One of these games was lawn tennis (Lawn Tennis Aprons, p. 128). ''As we have gone to the full length of adopting this English game, its special costume, low shoes and all, we have also made a place for the decorative apron which is introduced to give a touch of color and grace to the endless stripes that are worn'' (August 6, 1881). Riding habits were almost as stylized as a uniform. "For riding on horseback, ladies wear a skirt of the same length in front and behind, and narrow, since it only measures a yard and three-quarters around the bottom, and is entirely plain at the belt. There is not a single pleat in it, but only darts on the hips, like those used on waist, in order to mould the skirt closely to the form. As to the waist worn with habits, they are rather long and entirely plain basques, without any trimming whatever, the back alone being arranged in small fan pleats. With this is always worn a standing collar and cuffs of fine linen, a Surah neck-tie, and a tall hat with a dark blue veil" (April 30, 1881). The finest riding habits were made by English tailors, but those who could not afford these were able to have them made from patterns of the originals.

Special dress for bathing at the shore began around the middle of the nineteenth century (loose robes had been worn previously). By the late 1860s bathing was featured in the magazines every summer—but with some concern: "The plan of men and women bathing together at a public water-place is open to great objections, these innovations upon propriety are keeping many people with young daughters away from watering-places" (July 23, 1881). Another sport much enjoyed by Americans, judging by the number of illustrations devoted to it, was skating. For this ladies added a touch of festivity to their winter outfits and shortened their skirts to the ankle.

No costume was considered complete without a full complement of accessories. Morning, noon and night, both indoors and out, there was always something to put on the head, and, although there was only an occasional need for purses, hands had fans, parasols and muffs to occupy them. All accessories—gloves, handkerchiefs, hair ornaments, jewelry, aprons, shoes and stockings—provided surfaces to be decorated. None escaped the love of rich trimming.

Harper's Bazar had only peripheral interest in men's fashion. Children's clothes, however, were featured regularly. Little girls wore dresses resembling their mother's both in shape and adornments. Unlike today, most little boys also wore dresses or costumes with skirts. Even when they donned trousers at about the age of five, their costumes were not completely male —apparently their fashions were sexually ambiguous until early adolescence. Until one reached full maturity it was necessary to dress according to one's age. Almost all the illustrations of children's apparel carefully stated the age for which the costume was designed. For girls this generally involved the length of the skirt, shorter for the younger, longer for the older. For boys, after dresses, age determined the length and type of trousers and the degree of similarity to full-grown male attire. Infants' fashions changed very slowly, reflecting contemporary trends mainly in the sleeves. Narrow from the late 1860s, they became fuller, like those worn by their mothers, by the 1890s. Throughout the nineteenth century and well into the twentieth these little gowns, made with loving handstitches, were richly decorated with embroidery and laces.

Even though lingerie was completely concealed from public gaze, it changed with the times and was lavish with lace, embroidery, fancy tuckings and pale ribbons. Except for corsets and petticoats, underwear was made of either fine cotton or linen and was always white. The shape-makers, corsets and tournures or bustles, were expertly constructed to assist nature in producing the desired fashionable figure. Occasional movements to dispense with them were unsuccessful. Even children wore them (Corsets, p. 20). Reports by doctors of the time took full note of the deformed ribs and displaced digestive organs caused by this constriction. It would be interesting to know what behavioral psychologists would make of its effects on Victorian women.

Harper's Bazar addressed itself mainly to ladies whose households were staffed with servants. Not only were most of the fashions shown impractical for any sort of housework, but many of the gowns were so constructed that it would have been impossible for a woman to dress herself without assistance. Although female servants wore clothes similar to those of their mistresses, there was no danger that one would be mistaken for the other. Class consciousness was too strong to permit this. Somber colors, poorer fabrics stripped of trimmings along with a maid's or nurse's headdress would indicate the servant's station in society (Fig. m, Ladies' and Children's Summer Suits, pp. 44–45; Damassé Silk Evening Toilette, p. 122). Even when the apron was fashionable, there was a definite distinction between that which was worn for work and that which served as a decorative accessory for genteel occasions such as pouring tea (Aprons, p. 41).

Costumes and accessories can tell us a great deal about the fashions of the past, but hair styles too, are an integral part of fashion. Each cycle seemed to devise a coiffure to fit into its particular stylistic preferences. Posture—the structure on which fashion builds its form—is another facet of fashion. In the early 1870s the modish stance called the "Grecian Bend" thrust the upper part of the body forward head first, leaving the lower part swollen with puffs well back (Evening Toilettes, pp. 50, 72). After years of fairly natural verticality, posture again took a distorted appearance in the late 1890s. This time the head was held back while the rib cage was pushed forward to exaggerate the bosom into the much admired "pouter pigeon" silhouette (Cashmere Gown, p. 285).

The ideally fashionable face is perhaps the most subtle and difficult to define. Changing in mood, age and expression, it sums up the spirit of prevailing fashion in many ways. Fashion illustrations of 1867 show small, pretty faces. Innocent almost to the point of blankness, they are very much in keeping with the emphasis of the period on the beauty of inexperienced adolescence. As the nineteenth century moved toward its closing years, ideal features moved toward maturity. By the late 1890s, it was the well-developed, full-figured woman that the ladies were to pattern themselves after, and the face to go with this look was now adult and even showed a semblance of character and a cast of experience.

Because we participate in it daily, most of us are hardly aware that fashion produces a vocabulary of its own. Today we speak of the "hippie look" or talk about "bikinis" and "blue jeans." In the nineteenth century people had their own vocabulary to describe what they wore. Stemming from a period that tended to draw its creative inspiration from the past, many articles of dress were named after historic or lengendary figures.

American ladies who looked to France for their fashions also borrowed French words to name their clothes—even newly coined words were in the French manner. This produced descriptions which are as much period pieces as the costumes themselves. To preserve this flavor, and to add to the understanding and enjoyment of the fashions shown in this book, the captions for these plates are those which appeared with them in the original publication and, for the most part, retain their original spelling and punctuation. A glossary, p. 293, provides definitions of terms which may be unfamiliar to the modern reader.

❧ CONTENTS ❧

VICTORIAN
FASHIONS AND COSTUMES

FROM HARPER'S BAZAR

1867-1898

I

BUSTLES AND PUFFS

⤙ 1867-1874 ⤚

Sometimes fashions take their direction from practical needs. In the late 1860s, women became more involved in activities outside the home. Because the prevailing fashions, with their long, cumbersome, dirt-collecting trains, presented a hinderance, a "walking costume" emerged in 1866. Although it did not alter the general style, skirts were looped for freer movement, exposing ankle-length petticoats or underskirts. Interestingly enough, the caught-up skirts produced round puffs, giving the former conical silhouette a look reminiscent of that of the late eighteenth century (Walking Dresses, p. 4). The designers drew heavily from the fashions of that period (Promenade and Carriage Toilettes, p. 17). It was no accident that costumes were named after Dolly Varden, a heroine from *Barnaby Rudge,* a popular book by Charles Dickens set in the eighteenth century (Dolly Varden Walking Suit, p. 51).

The world of fashion was jolted in 1870. The Franco-Prussian War put a sudden end to the glittering Second Empire and the trend-setting court of the Emperor Napoleon III and the Empress Eugénie. During the war many of the French couturiers fled to Brussels, where they continued to work. Emmeline Raymond, *Harper's* "own correspondent" took to her heels and fled to Germany, but she was soon back at her post, reporting on French styles, and Paris once again dictated fashion.

Lacking a luxurious court to set styles, fashion turned to the theater, with its performers and fantasies, as a source of inspiration. In this process, fashion became increasingly more eclectic. Emulating the past, women dressed in costumes that might have been designed to be worn on the stage. Some appear to have been inspired by the Italian Renaissance (Fig. b, Street and Dinner Dresses, p. 16), others by painters such as Van Dyck (Opera Toilette, p. 47; Walking Dress, p. 61). Pendant sleeves similar to those popular in the late sixteenth and early seventeenth centuries were used (Visiting Toilette, p. 22). The shoulder mantle can be seen in Northern European paintings of the early seventeenth century (House Dress, p. 26; Visiting Toilette, p. 53; Spring Suit, p. 67). Chenille balls were used in an imitation of the lavish Elizabethan application of pearls (Evening Toilette, p. 62). Fashions of the period also have counterparts in the *Galerie des Modes et Costumes Français,* one of the earliest publications devoted primarily to fashion, printed in Paris, 1778–87 (Figs. a and c, Street and Dinner Dresses, p. 16; Walking Suit, p. 24; Sea-side Costume, p. 27; Evening Toilette, p. 63; Watering-place Costume, p. 66; Reception Dress and Carriage Dress, pp. 68–69).

There were also gowns that were pure confection. Looking like mounds of spun sugar candy, they were lavishly trimmed with artificial flowers, ribbons, etc. (Evening Toilettes, pp. 49, 71). By 1872, the trend toward freedom of movement was buried under a morass of drapery and trimmings. Late in 1874, surfeited by this massing and profusion, the silhouette began to compress to reveal the female torso (Walking Suit, p. 73; Worth Basque, p. 75).

The fashions of the 1860s had an aura of daintiness which also permeated accessories. Bonnets and hats were tiny. Little more than decorative headdresses, they seemed designed merely to blunt the point of the period's cone-shaped silhouette (Winter Bonnets, p. 5; Ladies' Wrappings pp. 14–15). Much of the lace that was lavished on costumes and accessories was very beautiful, and of the finest quality found in the nineteenth century (Promenade Toilettes, pp. 10, 19; Evening Toilette, p. 21; Bows, p. 32; Collars and Shoe Rosettes, p. 34).

Separates, which had been in wide use in the early 1860s, continued to be worn until the early 1870s. There were blouses and neckwear as delicate as infants' clothes (Hoop Skirts and Neck Accessories, p. 18), separate bodices to be combined with a variety of skirts, and a multitude of ties and bows for the neck and waist (Bodices, p. 35; Costumes and Lingerie, p. 48; Ornaments, p. 54). Outerwear consisted mainly of dolmans and hip-length jackets (Wraps, pp. 14–15, 42–43, 60). At times they matched the gowns over which they were worn, but they usually contrasted with them.

Like the laces, the jewelry of this period was of a high order. Pieces which have survived have become collector's items (Jewelry, p. 7). Toward the end of this fashion cycle, the gentle, rather delicate aspect of mid-Victoriana began to give way to a heavier, more obvious display of opulence.

3

d

c

b

a

WALKING DRESSES *(11.16.1867, p. 36).* **Fig. a:** costume of gray poplin. About three inches from the bottom, a shirr is run in the skirt and a cord passed through, which draws it up in gathers. Braid trimming of black

and rosette of velvet. Bonnet of lilac silk, with braided trimming. **Figs. c and d:** costume of black silk, with a broad trimming of black persane on the bottom of the skirt; the peplum and ends of the same material. The waist and

velvet. The paletot is trimmed with bias folds of the same stuff. Bonnet of gray silk. **Fig. b:** costume of lilac alpaca, with braided trimming of black velvet, like that of the preceding figure. Skirt looped up on each side with braid

peplum are fastened with jet buttons. Silk fringe and bead gimp complete the trimming.

WINTER BONNETS *(11.23.1867, p. 57).*
Fig. a: Lilia.
Fig. b: Trianon.
Fig. c: Marie Antoinette.
Fig. d: Fanchon.
Fig. e: Marie Stuart.
Fig. f: duchesse.
Fig. g: universal.
Fig. h: imperial.
Fig. i: evening coiffure à la Premier Empire.
Fig. j: cap coiffure.

TRAVELING PALETOT; FRONT AND BACK *(4.25.1868, p. 404).*

JEWELRY *(5.16.1868, p. 453)* from Messrs. Tiffany & Co. and Browne & Spaulding, New York.

Figs. a–e: diamond and emerald parure consisting of ring, necklace, brooch, ear-rings and bracelet.

Fig. f: diamond, emerald, sapphire, opal and pearl brooch and ear-rings.

Fig. g: diamond brooch or pendant for necklace and ear-rings.

C. DELHOMME.

COUNTRY TOILETTES (*6.13.1868, p. 521*). **Fig. a:** dress of light gray silk, with double skirt. The trimming consists of ruches of the same material as the dress, folds of gray satin and gray silk-covered rosettes and tassels. Belt of gray satin. **Fig. b:** dress of blue poplin, with narrow ruche of the same material; bias folds of blue satin and blue silk fringe. Belt with sash of the same material as the dress, and trimmed to match. **Fig. c:** dress and paletot of brown gros grain. The trimming consists of brown satin binding and brown satin buttons. **Fig. d:** dress of gray alpaca trimmed with bias folds of gray satin; buttons, fringe, tassels and small gray buckles. **Fig. e:** dress of brown poult de soie, trimmed with brown silk cord, buttons, tassels, and fringe of the color of the dress.

a   b   c   d   e

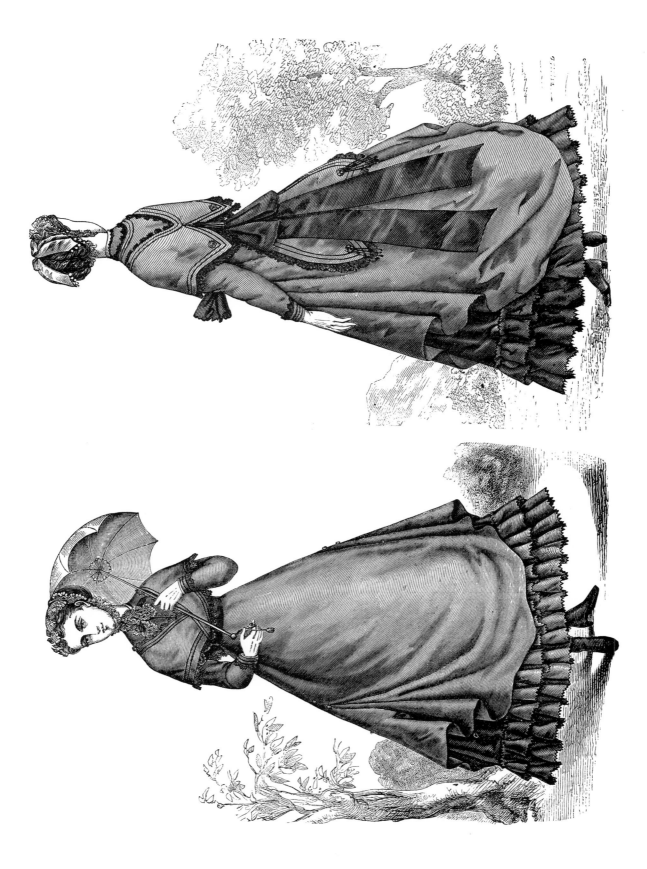

STREET DRESS WITH BASHLIK FICHU; FRONT AND BACK (*7.4.1868, cover*).

a *b* *c* *d* *e*

PROMENADE TOILETTES *(7.11.1868, cover).* **Fig. a:** round dress and scarf mantilla of lilac foulard, embroidered with violet silk. Lilac crape bonnet, trimmed with lace. **Fig. b:** under-skirt of blue and white striped foulard.

Short over-skirt, looped up by means of two lapels, and scarf fichu of blue and white figured alpaca, trimmed with a pinked frill of blue silk. White lace bonnet. **Fig. c:** round dress and polonaise of Sultan red foulard, with

skirt embroidered round the bottom and polonaise round the edge with silk of the same color. Rice straw toquet, trimmed with a small white bird and fall of white grenadine. **Fig. d:** dress of light green silk, with long lace paletot

with flowing sleeves. Black lace bonnet, trimmed with green ribbon. **Fig. e:** lavender silk dress, with black lace over-skirt and Marie Antoinette fichu. Black lace bonnet, trimmed with lavender ribbon.

CHILDREN'S SEA-SIDE COSTUMES (8.29.1868, p. 697). **Fig. a:** polonaise toilette of striped foulard for girl seven years old. Mantilla of white cloth, trimmed with galloon to match the dress. Royal hat trimmed with blue ribbon. **Fig. b:** Hungarian costume for boy two years old of nankeen trimmed with black velvet with velvet belt. Black velvet

cap and feather. **Fig. c:** under-skirt and waist of crimson and white striped percale, for young girl fifteen years old. Waist trimmed with bretelles and sailor collar. Over-skirt of dark brown Corinth cloth, short and looped up behind with a bow. **Fig. d:** dress for girl eight years old. Under-skirt and waist of sky-blue China silk. Short tunic of white Floren-

tine, caught up at the sides with a rosette. Sash of blue China silk. Florentine hat of rice straw, trimmed with a cluster of roses. **Fig. e:** dress for a girl nine years old. Skirt and waist of light brown mozambique with two rows of quilled flounces around the bottom of the skirt. Marie Antoinette fichu of white muslin, confined at the waist by a knot of green ribbon.

Prince of Wales toque, trimmed with ribbons. **Fig. f:** country costume for boy six years old. Blouse and panteloons of French cloth buttoned up the sides with pearl buttons. Leather belt. Hat of same material as the dress.

CHILDREN'S COUNTRY TOILETTES (8.29.1868. p. 697). **Fig. a:** dress for girl six years old of white foulard striped with blue. Waist with bretelles, trimmed with pleated blue ribbon. Short sleeves. Tucked muslin under-waist, trimmed with needle-work insertion, with sleeves of the same. Blue satin Français gaiter, with pearl buttons. **Fig. b:** dress of toile écru for young girl fourteen years old, trimmed on the bottom with a pleated flounce, over which is set white galloon. Marie-Antoinette pelerine-fichu, rounded in the back and broad rounded ends, the whole trimmed with a pleated flounce, confined by white galloon. Maroon straw toque, with a black figured lace scarf wound round the crown and knotted behind. Linen under-waist

with sleeves. Kid gaiters of the same color as the dress. **Fig. c:** dress of Scotch poplin for girl five years old, trimmed round the bottom with three rows of narrow cherry velvet. Small scutcheon-shaped pocket, edged with cherry velvet. Scotch poplin corsage with jacket cut straight behind and reaching only to the waist, and also bordered in cherry velvet. Linen collar and cuffs. English straw hat, trimmed with black velvet and wild flowers. Short white stockings. Black kid boots. **Fig. d:** costume for boy six years old. Pleated skirt of light merino blue French cloth, trimmed down the sides with bows of blue gros grain. Jacket with small pockets banded with galloon, each strip of galloon being studded with silver lozenge. Wide linen

collar. Boating hat, trimmed with blue ribbon. **Fig. e:** costume for girl eight years old. Dress of pink silk, cut square in the neck, and trimmed with pleating of the same. Short sleeves, trimmed in the same manner. Pink silk sash, with large bow, and ends terminating with a bow. Tucked muslin under-waist, with sleeves and embroidered cuffs. Pearl gray satin Français gaiters. **Fig. f:** boating costume for boy from eight to ten years old. Light gray poplin blouse, confined round the waist by a patent leather belt. Wide collar of the same material as the blouse, with an anchor embroidered in the corners. Full trowsers reaching to the knee. Red stockings. **Fig. g:** dress for young girl twelve years old. Skirt of mauve silk, covered with white muslin skirt

with small tucks and insertion trimming. Tunic simulated by points embroidered on muslin and surmounted with insertion, with medallions embroidered above the points. Waist cut square in the neck, and trimmed with points of embroidered muslin. Mauve silk bows on the shoulders. Bow of wide mauve ribbon with long ends fastened to the belt. Rice straw hat, trimmed with a wreath of blue-bells. **Fig. h:** dress for boy four years old. Trowsers of toile écru, trimmed with narrow coral-colored worsted galloon. Jacket trimmed with the same. Tucked linen shirt. Russia leather boots.

a *b* *c* *d*

DIFFERENT SKATING COSTUMES (2.6.1869, cover). **Fig. a:** dress of dark gray corduroy with fur trimming. The upper skirt is looped on the side and trimmed with a bow. The paletot is of black velvet with a fur border, and is finished with a black satin sash trimmed with fringe. Black velvet hat with lace ends.

Fig. b: Hungarian suit. The trowsers, short dress, and paletot are of black velveteen, trimmed with kimmer. The trowsers are pleated and bound at the ankle. Round hat with black velvet revers, trimmed with an ostrich feather and velvet rosette. Gloves of Danish leather trimmed with fur. High boots

with fur trimming. **Fig. c:** polonaise trowsers and paletot of dark blue cloth trimmed with gray Astrakhan. Gray Astrakhan muff and boa. Toque of dark blue cloth trimmed with Astrakhan. High boots trimmed with fur. **Fig. d:** dress of garnet cloth. The under skirt is trimmed with a flounce, and the upper one

is looped up in the manner shown in the illustration. Paletot and muff are of garnet cloth trimmed with rabbit fur. Black velvet hat with ostrich feather. High Russian boots.

a   b   c   d   e   f

j   k   l   m   n   o

g   h   i

p   q   r

LADIES' SPRING AND SUMMER WRAP-PINGS *(5.15.1869, pp. 312–313).*
Fig. a: Bordeaux paletot.
Figs. b and c: Marie Antoinette fichu, front and back.
Figs. d and e: Montpensier paletot, front and back.
Figs. f and g: Don Parasol paletot, back and front.
Figs. h and i: valentine paletot, back and front.
Fig. j: Hélène paletot, back.
Fig. k: talma for elderly lady.
Fig. l: Anne Boleyn paletot, back.
Fig. m: Hélène paletot, front.
Fig. n: Anne Boleyn paletot, front.
Fig. o: Fanchonnette mantelet, back.
Fig. p: Ella mantelet, front.
Fig. q: Fanchonnette mantelet, front.
Fig. r: Ella mantelet, back.

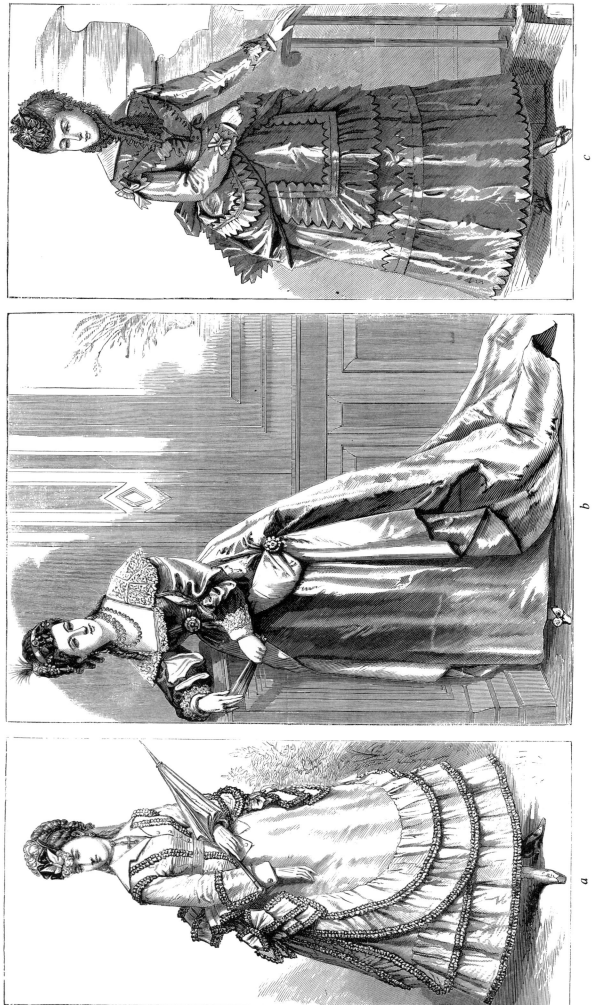

a

b

c

STREET AND DINNER DRESSES (*6.5.1869, p. 356*). **Fig. a:** short walking dress. Suit of blue foulard. Short under-skirt, trimmed with two flounces of the same material as the dress. Over-skirt rounded up at the sides, where it is finished with two large bows, and trimmed with two similar flounces. White linen vest, with broad rolling collar. Short jacket of blue foulard, edged with a ruche of mauve ribbon,

open in front and belted with a mauve sash and ends. Mauve hat, with white feather and butterfly. Mauve parasol. **Fig. b:** dinner dress. Under dress of green gros grain, just long enough to clear the floor, with low corsage. Court mantle of the same material, lined with white, with long train, and turned back and fastened in front, with a rosette of gold and brown ribbon. Belt of gold and brown ribbon, closed in front by a rosette. The man-

tle has full sleeves, open all the way down, and caught together at the elbow and wrist over an under-sleeve. Cuffs and broad collar of rich lace. Necklace of coral beads and coral ornaments; gold band and aigrette in the hair. **Fig. c:** street dress. Suit of rich bronze poplin. Skirt trimmed on the bottom with deep scalloped flounce, surmounted with a rather broad bias fold and a scalloped strip of poplin, the scallops pointing upward. Tablier trimmed in

the same manner, with scalloped flounce and bias fold. Adjusted casaque, with bretelle trimming, panier, and sash and ends with scalloped edges. Light green gloves. Broad linen collar. Black lace hat, trimmed with Marguerite and yellow wild flowers. Bronze parasol. Bronze boots.

PROMENADE AND CARRIAGE TOI-
LETTES (7.17.1869, p. 461). **Fig. a:** walking
dress of buff pongee. The skirt is trimmed
on the bottom with three full flounces of white
guipure, set on straight, and headed with a
pinked ruche of green silk. A fourth guipure
flounce forms arabesques in the manner
shown in the illustration. The casaque is scalloped round the bottom, and bouffant behind,
and is trimmed with white guipure and green
ruches. Buff pongee parasol, lined with green.
White lace hat, trimmed with a large red rose
and buds. Rose in the low corsage, underneath which a puffing of lace is worn. Rose-
colored gloves. **Fig. b:** carriage or visiting
dress of coral and white foulard. The trailing
skirt is trimmed with two deep scalloped
flounces of coral silk, set one a little way above
the other: these flounces slope up in front to
make room for several rounding flounces of
the striped foulard, to simulate an under-skirt.
Adjusted casaque of coral and white striped
foulard, trimmed around the bottom with a
double scalloped flounce of coral silk. Sash
with large fan bow and ends of coral silk;
the ends are trimmed with two scalloped
flounces. The neck, armholes, and wrists of
the casaque are finished with a coral silk
ruche. White lace hat with coral ostrich tufts.
Wrought gold jewelry. Straw-colored gloves.
White parasol lined with pink.

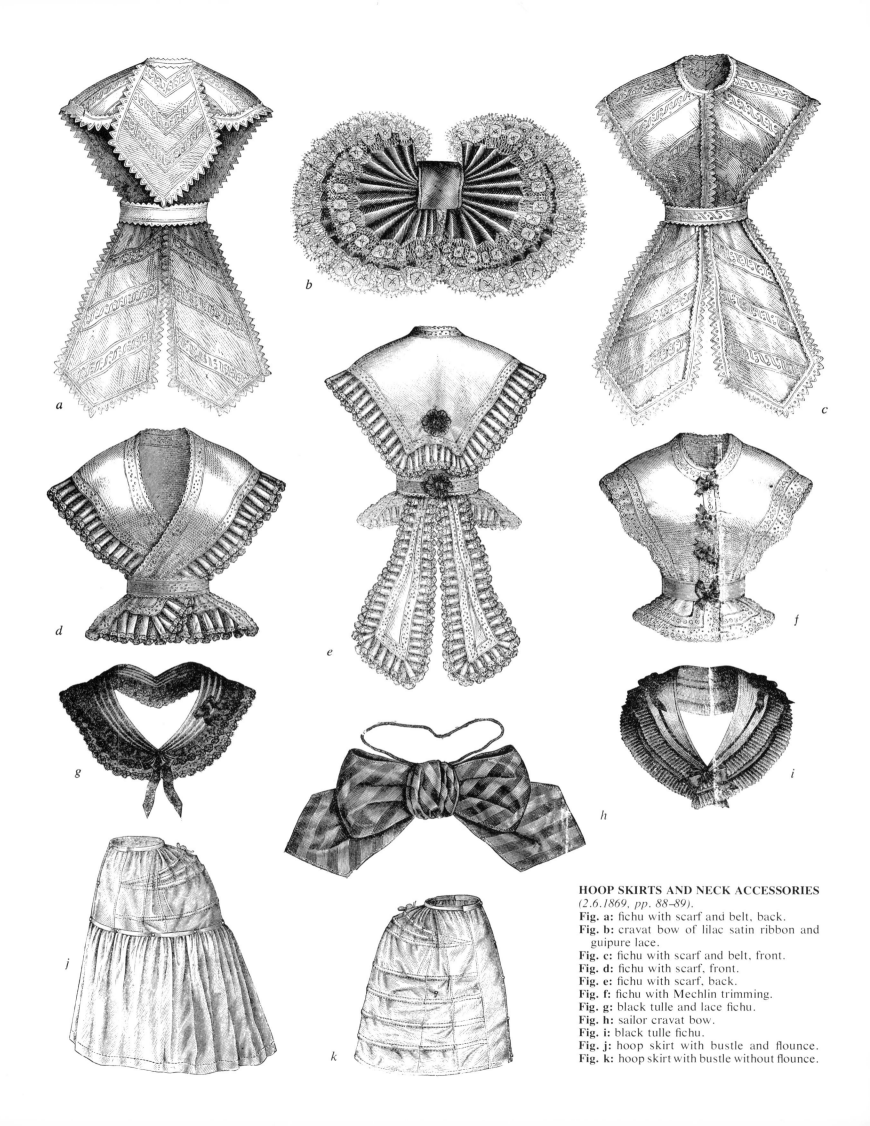

HOOP SKIRTS AND NECK ACCESSORIES
(2.6.1869, pp. 88–89).
Fig. a: fichu with scarf and belt, back.
Fig. b: cravat bow of lilac satin ribbon and guipure lace.
Fig. c: fichu with scarf and belt, front.
Fig. d: fichu with scarf, front.
Fig. e: fichu with scarf, back.
Fig. f: fichu with Mechlin trimming.
Fig. g: black tulle and lace fichu.
Fig. h: sailor cravat bow.
Fig. i: black tulle fichu.
Fig. j: hoop skirt with bustle and flounce.
Fig. k: hoop skirt with bustle without flounce.

PROMENADE TOILETTE *(7.31.1869, p. 493)*. The short dress is of écru crêpe de Chine, with an over-skirt of the same, edged with a broad box-pleated trimming of blue silk. Square low corsage, and short sleeves. Lace sacque, looped at the side with a blue rosette, and belted with a wide blue ribbon sash, with a large bow and ends. Yellow straw hat, which is scarcely more than a diadem, fastened round the chignon of curls by an elastic. Écru pongee parasol covered with black lace. Blue gaiters, laced in front, and trimmed with an écru rosette.

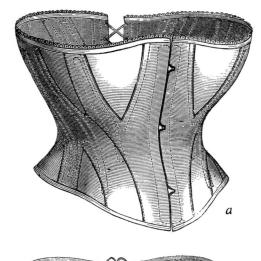

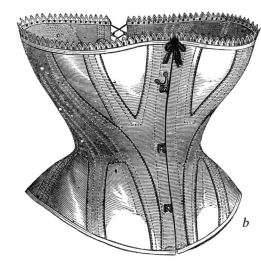

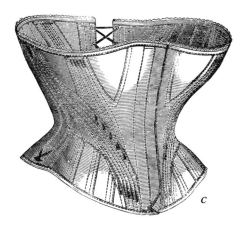

a

b

c

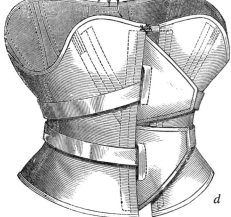

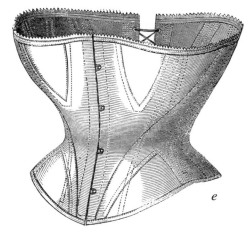

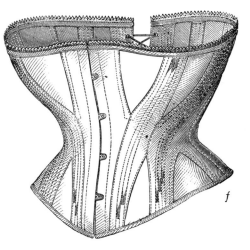

d

e

f

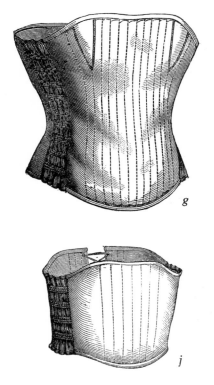

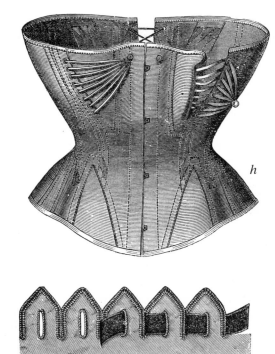

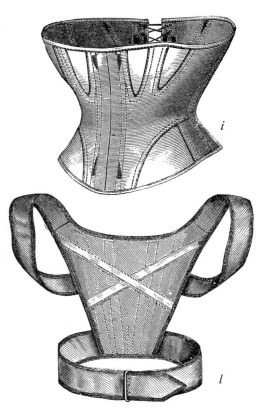

g

h

i

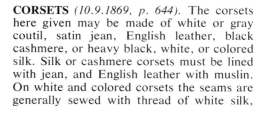

j

k

l

CORSETS *(10.9.1869, p. 644).* The corsets here given may be made of white or gray coutil, satin jean, English leather, black cashmere, or heavy black, white, or colored silk. Silk or cashmere corsets must be lined with jean, and English leather with muslin. On white and colored corsets the seams are generally sewed with thread of white silk,

while black corsets are sewed with red silk.

Fig. a: short corset of white coutil.
Fig. b: long corset of white coutil.
Fig. c: English leather short corset.
Fig. d: negligé corset.
Fig. e: short satin jean corset for elderly lady.
Fig. f: short corset of gray coutil.
Fig. g: corset for girl from 8 to 10 years old.

Fig. h: long corset of gray coutil with shirr.
Fig. i: corset for girl from 12 to 14 years old.
Fig. j: corset for child from 1 to 2 years old.
Fig. k: trimming for white coutil long corset.
Fig. l: shoulder braces for girl from 8 to 10 years old.

EVENING TOILETTE *(2.19.1870, cover).* Skirt of pink-coral gros grain, trimmed with three pinked flounces of the same material, which extend up the front. Over-skirt of point lace, draped behind *en panier* by means of two gros grain ribbons of the same shade as the dress, tied in a bow. Basque corsage of pink coral gros grain, with vandyked bertha, opening in front over a white lace underwaist, and confined by a cluster of pink roses. Wreath of pink roses and leaves in the hair. Necklace of pearl beads, with pink coral medallion. Pink coral and pearl bracelets.

VISITING TOILETTE (*6.11.1870, cover*). Suit of *ciel*-blue poult de soie, embroidered with silk of a darker shade. The skirt just clears the ground in front and has a long trail. The trimming of the skirt and mantle consists of a pleating of rose-pink gauze, with a puffed heading. The waist is heart-shaped and worn over a chemisette of puffed lace. The sleeve is straight to the elbow, and terminates in a large puff, with two wide frills of white Duchesse lace, falling over the hand, and another narrower one over the puff. Each frill is finished with a pink silk bow. The Fon-

tanges mantle is trimmed like the skirt, and is pleated on the left shoulder, and box-pleated under the arm. It is ornamented on the left shoulder with a pink silk bow, with fringed ends, and is carried round to the right hip, where it is fastened and looped with a pink bow. White chip hat, trimmed with rose-pink flowers and crêpe de Chine of the same color. Boots of the shade of the dress. Straw-color kid gloves. DESCRIPTION OF CUT PAPER PATTERN OF VISITING TOILETTE: This cut pattern consists of three pieces, viz., Trained skirt, waist, and Fontanges mantle. *Trained*

Skirt. The skirt is in five pieces: Front breadth, two gored side breadths, and two straight back breadths; and is put together as notched. Quantity of material, 24 inches wide, 13 yards. *Waist*. This is in five pieces: front, back, side, sleeve, and puff. Bust measure, 40 inches. Quantity of material, 24 inches wide, 3 yards. *Fontanges Mantle*. This mantle is in one piece, half of which is given in the pattern, and is sewed in with the waist. Quantity of material, 24 inches wide, 13 yards.

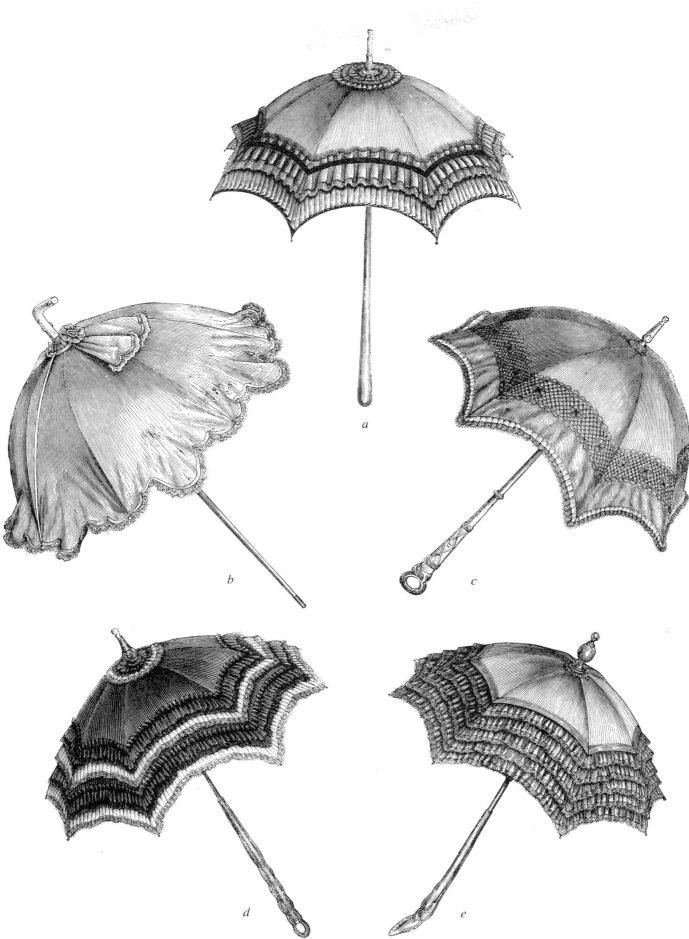

PARASOLS *(6.18.1870, p. 392).*
Fig. a: fawn-colored silk parasol.

Fig. b: corn-colored silk travelling parasol.
Fig. c: light brown silk parasol.

Fig. d: black poult de soie parasol.
Fig. e: gray poult de soie parasol.

WALKING SUIT *(6.25.1870, cover)*. This pretty suit consists of a walking skirt, tunic, and basque waist, with revers collar. The walking skirt is of lilac silk, trimmed on the bottom with two ruches of the same material. The tunic is of violet silk, pointed on the sides and open in the back, with an apron front, and is edged with a ruche of lilac silk. The Pompadour basque waist of violet silk is worn over a plain waist of lilac silk. The flowing sleeves of the under-waist and the basque waist are edged with lilac silk ruche. The basque waist may, however, be made high necked, with trimming set on to simulate a Pompadour waist. Linen collar, formed of three revers overlapping each other. These revers may be made of the same material as the dress, and cut in one piece, in three points.

Lace under-sleeves. Violet silk hat, with lilac feathers. Lilac gloves. Lilac boots.

COIFFURES AND SUITS FOR CHILDREN FROM 1 TO 12 YEARS OLD *(7.2.1870, cover)*. **Fig. a:** dress with gray alpaca bodice for girl from 10 to 12 years old. This dress is trimmed with black velvet and has a scarf of gray alpaca. Blouse waist of Swiss muslin. Part hair in the middle, comb back, and arrange in two braids. Fasten a bow of ribbon to the end of each braid. Tyrolese hat of black straw, trimmed with black gros grain ribbon and cock's feathers. **Fig. b:** dress and blouse waist of blue and white foulard for girl from 9 to 11 years old. Make bretelles of blue silk, bind the edges with blue satin, and trim the scallops with blue silk fringe. Make belt and

fan-shaped bow with blue silk. Black velvet ribbon for the neck. Part the hair in the middle, comb back, and arrange in two braids, which must be pinned high, in the manner shown in the illustration. Black straw hat, trimmed with black gros grain ribbon and a white ostrich feather. **Fig. c:** dress with bodice of gray pongee for girl from 9 to 11 years old. The trimming of this dress consists of a bias strip of the material bound on both sides with blue silk. On the shoulders and front of the waist bows of blue ribbon. Make belt and scarf of the same ribbon. Cut the waist of the material and muslin lining. A blouse waist of pleated Swiss muslin, the neck of which is trimmed with a ruche made of two rows of lace box-pleated, completes the costume. Arrange the hair in curls, and tie blue silk

ribbon in it. **Fig. d:** suit for boy from 2 to 4 years old. Make this suit of dark blue navy cloth, and trim and bind with black silk braid. Black buttons and silk cord loops close the jacket. Under waist with sailor collar, edged with dimity ruffle. Comb hair back from the face. Hat of yellow English straw, trimmed with ribbon bows and feathers. **Fig. e:** dress for girls 6 to 8 years old. This dress is made of brown silk serge, and has a square neck. Trim the neck and cuffs with pinked ruche of the material. Chemisette of pleated Swiss muslin, with collar of Swiss muslin, insertion and lace. Black velvet ribbon for the neck. Crimp the hair, comb back, and let it hang down. Tie a brown velvet ribbon around the head. **Fig. f:** jacket for girl from 1 to 3 years old. This jacket is of light brown merino, and

is trimmed with a bias band of dark brown merino bound with brown satin. Bind the cuffs with satin. Comb the hair back, arrange in two braids, and to the ends of the braids fasten a bow. **Fig. g:** suit for girl 7 to 9 years old. The dress is of blue poplin with an over dress of gray poplin. The front of the over dress is cut diagonally, and trimmed with bias strips of blue poplin. Summer bashlik of white cashmere trimmed with black velvet ribbon. Part the hair in the middle, arrange in two braids, and wind about the head like a diadem. **Fig. h:** jacket for girl from 9 to 10 years old. This jacket is made of white velveteen, trimmed with revers and buttons of red velvet. The hair is parted in the middle, arranged in two braids, and pinned up high. Hat of white English straw trimmed with green leaves.

Fig. i: low-necked dress for girl from 3 to 5 years old. This dress is of white piqué with a ruffle two inches wide, laid in flat pleats. Set the bottom of the short puffed sleeves into an embroidered band. High-necked blouse waist of pleated Swiss muslin. Comb the hair back, and confine it with a blue gros grain ribbon. **Fig. j:** suit for girl from 8 to 10 years old. This dress is of light gray poplin, and has a high-necked waist. Gray straw hat with gray gauze scarf and spray of blue flowers. The hair is parted in the middle, arranged in two braids, and pinned high.

TRAINED HOUSE DRESS (*7.23.1870, cover*). This dress may be made in grenadine, Chambery gauze, foulard, pongee, silk, China crape, or any fabric except thin muslins. The original is made of white foulard. The two back breadths of the skirt are trimmed to the waist with flounces of Bruges lace. The side and front breadths are trimmed around the bottom and up the side of the third seam to the waist with a ruche of gros grain four inches wide, pinked on each edge in small points, and two others, an inch and a half wide, with two inches space between. The wide ruche and upper ruche are violet, and the middle one green. Long lilac sash in the back, with rosette bow, edged with Bruges lace. Plain waist, square in front, and an inch and a half lower in the back of the neck than an ordinary waist. Ruches an inch wide trim the edge of the neck, and pass over the arm-hole and down the front and the back to form the shape, the lower one being violet and the upper one green. The coat-sleeve is trimmed diagonally with green and violet ruches an inch and a half wide. The page sleeve is trimmed the entire length with a ruche three and a half inches wide, and two others an inch wide and upper ruches being violet, and the middle one green. The neck and sleeves are edged with Bruges lace. Violet ribbon in hair. Gold necklace with enameled medallion and enameled earrings. DESCRIPTION OF CUT PATTERN OF TRAINED HOUSE DRESS: this pattern comprises two articles, viz.; plain waist with coat and page sleeves, and eight-gored trained skirt. *Plain Waist With Sleeves*. This pattern is in five parts, viz. front, side piece, back, coat-sleeve, and long page sleeve. Quantity of material, 24 inches wide, 4 yards. Ruching when made, 12 yards. *Eight-Gored Trained Skirt*. This pattern is in six pieces: two straight back breadths, two side gores, gored front breadth, and belt. The train is three-quarters of a yard long. Quantity of material, 24 inches wide, 12 yards. Ruching, when made, 12 yards. Lace, 14 yards.

SEA-SIDE COSTUME *(8.6.1870, cover)*. This picturesque costume may be made of any thick material, such as foulard, silk, challie, yak cloth, beaver, mohair, pongee, etc., and trimmed with silk or velvet in colors to suit the taste. Écru, tourterelle gray, and lavender, trimmed with maroon, blue, and black make fine contrasts. In the original the skirt is of gold-colored foulard, trimmed with black velvet and buttons. Plain pointed waist of gold-colored foulard, trimmed with two rows of buttons of the same color, with coat-sleeves trimmed with black velvet. Linen sailor collar. A sleeveless polka jacket of purple silk, with black velvet trimming. White crêpe de Chine scarf. Black velvet hat, with cockade of purple ribbon, and gold and white feathers. Purple gloves. Black boots. Écru staff parasol, with black velvet trimming.

a   b   c   d   e   f   g

l   m   n   o   p

h   *i*   *j*   *k*

r   *s*   *t*   *u*

LADIES' AND CHILDREN'S WALKING, HOUSE, AND EVENING DRESSES *(8.27.1870, pp. 552–553).*

Fig. a: dress for girl from 8 to 10 years old.

Fig. b: écru foulard walking dress.

Fig. c: gray foulard walking dress.

Fig. d: traveling dress for young girl.

Fig. e: white piqué dress for girl from 2 to 4 years old.

Fig. f: dress for girl from 6 to 8 years old.

Fig. g: buff linen princesse dress.

Fig. h: gray poult de soie dress with lace casaque.

Fig. i: dress with sacque for girl from 3 to 5 years old.

Fig. j: lilac mohair walking dress.

Fig. k: violet silk dress with black gros grain paletot.

Fig. l: gray mohair walking dress.

Fig. m: buff pongee walking dress.

Fig. n: gray foulard dress with green satin trimming.

Fig. o: gray silk dress with basque.

Fig. p: pink silk and crêpe de chine ball or evening dress.

Fig. q: black gros grain walking dress.

Fig. r: suit for boy from 2 to 4 years old.

Fig. s: gray linen dress for girl from 10 to 12 years old.

Fig. t: light gray foulard walking dress with violet silk trimming.

Fig. u: écru foulard dress with tunic.

a   *b*   *c*   *d*

BRIDAL TOILETTES AND GIRL'S DRESS
(8.27.1870, cover). **Fig. a:** dress for girl from
5 to 7 years old. Under-skirt of white alpaca,
trimmed with a wide pleated flounce of the
same. Draped upper skirt and bodice of blue
mozambique, trimmed with pinked blue silk
ruches. Bands and bows also of blue silk.
White alpaca blouse trimmed with folds of
the same. Italian straw hat, trimmed with

black velvet and corn flowers. **Fig. b:** bridal
dress with rounded waist. Dress of white
poult de soie with rounded neck. Trim the
neck and sleeves with pleating of the material.
Chemisette of pleated Mechlin. Long blonde
veil, and orange wreath with long sprays falling over the back. Bouquet of orange flowers.
Fig. c: Swiss muslin bridal dress. This dress
consists of a skirt, square-necked waist, belt,

and basque. It is made of fine Swiss muslin,
and is trimmed with pleated ruffles of the
same, and folds and bows of white silk. **Fig. d:**
white satin bridal dress. Dress with high-
necked basque waist of white satin, trimmed
with satin folds and Valenciennes lace. Long
white blond veil and orange sprays.

PASSEMENTERIE AND CROCHET TRIM-MINGS FOR WINTER WRAPPINGS.
(11.19.1870, p. 749).
Fig. a: crochet edging.
Fig. b: silk cord edging.

Fig. c: silk cord agrafe.
Fig. d: silk cord agrafe.
Fig. e: silk cord agrafe with tassels.
Fig. f: silk cord agrafe with grelot tassels.
Fig. g: silk cord agrafe with silk tassels.

Fig. h: silk and twist bead button.
Fig. i: cord and bugle button.
Fig. j: crochet and jet button.
Fig. k: crochet button.

BOWS *(2.11.1871, p. 85).*
Fig. a: green gros grain cravat bow.
Fig. b: granite crêpe de chine cravat bow.
Fig. c: black gauze cravat bow.
Fig. d: black gauze cravat bow.
Fig. e: cravat bow.
Fig. f: velvet and satin bow for the hair.

Fig. g: velvet and moiré antique bow for the hair.
Fig. h: violet satin and black velvet cravat bow.
Fig. i: scarlet gros grain cravat bow.
Fig. j: blue gros grain cravat bow.

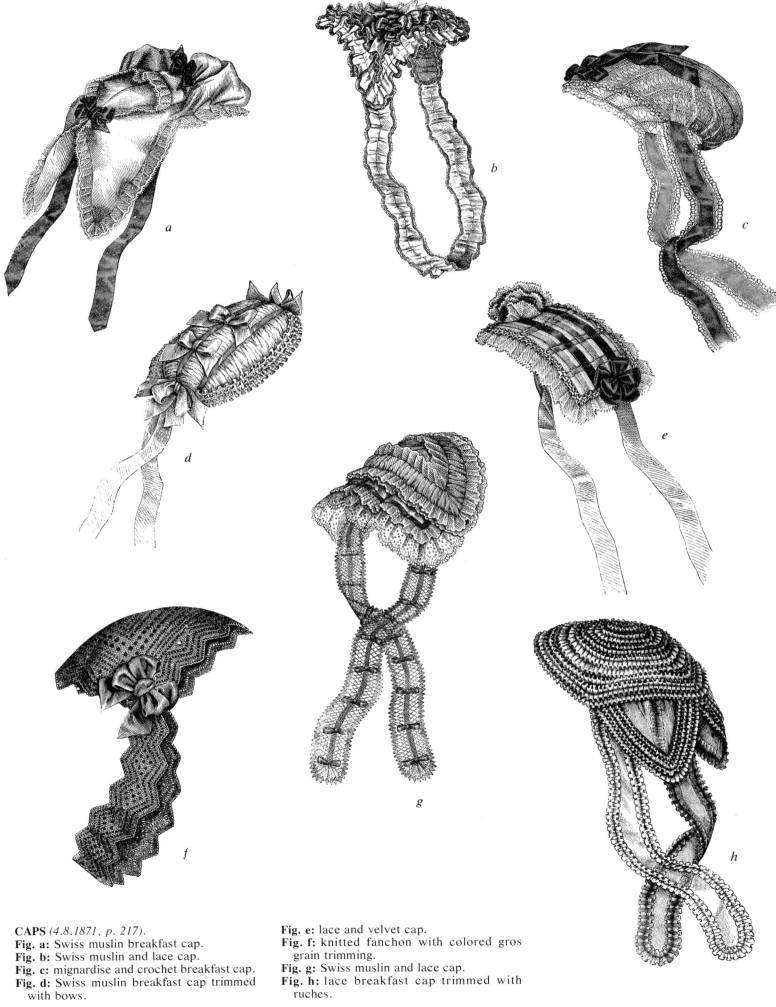

CAPS *(4.8.1871, p. 217).*

Fig. a: Swiss muslin breakfast cap.
Fig. b: Swiss muslin and lace cap.
Fig. c: mignardise and crochet breakfast cap.
Fig. d: Swiss muslin breakfast cap trimmed with bows.

Fig. e: lace and velvet cap.
Fig. f: knitted fanchon with colored gros grain trimming.
Fig. g: Swiss muslin and lace cap.
Fig. h: lace breakfast cap trimmed with ruches.

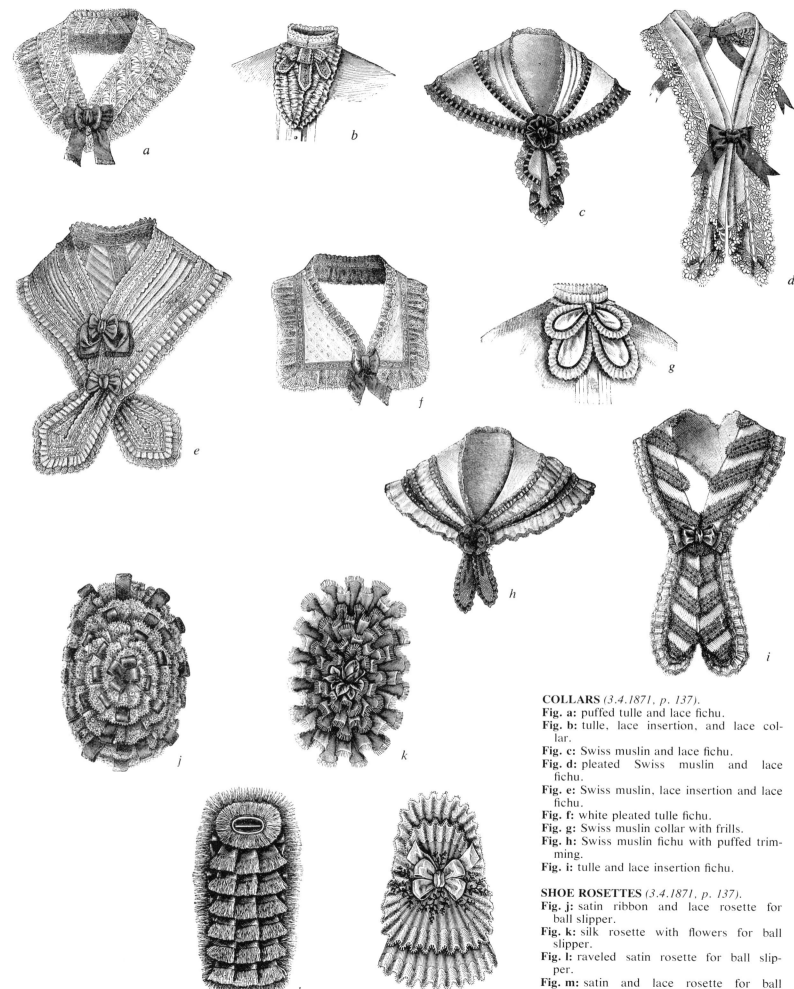

COLLARS *(3.4.1871, p. 137)*.

Fig. a: puffed tulle and lace fichu.

Fig. b: tulle, lace insertion, and lace collar.

Fig. c: Swiss muslin and lace fichu.

Fig. d: pleated Swiss muslin and lace fichu.

Fig. e: Swiss muslin, lace insertion and lace fichu.

Fig. f: white pleated tulle fichu.

Fig. g: Swiss muslin collar with frills.

Fig. h: Swiss muslin fichu with puffed trimming.

Fig. i: tulle and lace insertion fichu.

SHOE ROSETTES *(3.4.1871, p. 137)*.

Fig. j: satin ribbon and lace rosette for ball slipper.

Fig. k: silk rosette with flowers for ball slipper.

Fig. l: raveled satin rosette for ball slipper.

Fig. m: satin and lace rosette for ball slipper.

GROS GRAIN WALKING DRESS WITH
VELVET CASAQUE *(3.4.1872, p. 137).* Fig. n.

BODICES *(3.4.1871, p. 137).*
Fig. o: low waist with puffed trimming.
Fig. p: low waist with box-pleated trim-
    ming.
Fig. q: basque-waist with revers.
Fig. r: basque-waist with heart-shaped neck.
Fig. s: basque-waist with chemise Russe.

a

b

c

d

WINTER HATS AND BONNETS WITH FRAMES *(2.18.1871, p. 105)*. **Fig. a:** this gray felt hat is trimmed with loops and ends of gray gros grain ribbon and light gray feathers. **Fig. b:** this brown velvet bonnet is trimmed with loops and ends of the material and of brown gros grain, dark brown and light brown feathers, and black lace. Velvet strings. **Fig. c:** this black felt hat is trimmed with loops and ends of black gros grain ribbon, a spray of flowers, and black lace. **Fig. d:** this blue velvet bonnet is trimmed with loops of the same, a blue and a white feather, white illusion strings, and white lace.

HAIR DRESSING FOR YOUNG LADIES *(3.25.1871, cover)*. **Figs. a–c:** coiffure of long hair. To arrange this coiffure part the hair in the middle from forehead to the neck, and also part the hair from ear to ear. On each side of the middle parting divide the front hair into two parts. Crimp the two portions of the front next the middle parting by putting it up on crimping pins, then arrange it, as shown in the illustration, so that it falls over the forehead. Comb the remainder of the front hair up over the crimped hair, twist the strands together for a length of about an inch, and fasten them with hair-pins for the present, leaving the ends hang loose. Now comb down the right half of the back hair, and arrange it in a three-strand braid together with the ends of the front hair of the right side (see Fig. c). Comb the left half of the back hair

upward, as shown by Fig. c; tie it with a string, and arrange it in a three-strand braid together with the ends of the front hair of the left side. In arranging this braid, it is to be remembered that it is afterward laid around the head as a bandeau. Now remove the string with which the hair of the left side was tied, and fasten the end of the right braid under the beginning of the left braid, so that the right braid lies in the neck, as shown by Fig. b. Bring the left braid over the front of the head as shown by Fig. a, and fasten the end under the beginning of the right braid. Secure the braids in this position with hair-pins. Finish the coiffure with a bow of colored ribbon, as shown by the illustration. **Figs. d and e:** coiffure of short hair. To arrange this coiffure, part the hair,

as for Fig. f, from ear to ear, and part the front hair in the middle; arrange it so as to fall over the front of the forehead, and comb it back at the sides. Comb the ends of the front hair down together with the back hair. Cover the parting between the front and back hair with a tortoise-shell band. **Fig. f:** coiffure with crimped chignon of hair of a medium length. To arrange this coiffure, divide the hair, first, from ear to ear, and then part the front hair in the middle. Put up the hair on crimping pins, and leave it so for eight or ten hours; or, if there is not time for this, friz it. Now take down the hair (Fig. e shows the manner of putting up the hair on pins, and also several crimped strands), comb out the back hair, and tie it tightly together with a string four inches above the ends. Bring the ends together on the inside, lay the strings closely about the head, and tie them on the top of the head between the front and back hair; the hair's ends must come inside of the chignon thus formed. Comb the front hair back, as shown by the illustration, and roll the ends under so as to conceal them. When the hair is thin, both the chignon and front hair may be arranged over rolls. Finally, fasten a tortoise-shell band on the front of the head in such a manner that the front hair falls on the forehead in small puffs.

a   *b*   *c*   *d*

e   *f*   *g*

LADIES' DINNER DRESSES, AND SUIT FOR BOY FROM 4 TO 6 YEARS OLD *(3.25.1871, p. 184).*

Fig. a: dress with double skirt and basque-waist.

Fig. b: dress with basque-waist for elderly lady.

Fig. c: dress with Swiss muslin over-skirt and blouse-waist.

Fig. d: dress with train and heart-shaped basque-waist.

Fig. e: suit for boy 4 to 6 years old.

Fig. f: evening dress for young lady.

Fig. g: dress with double skirt and heart-shaped basque-waist.

SPRING AND SUMMER SUITS FOR BOYS AND GIRLS FROM THREE TO FOURTEEN YEARS OLD *(4.22.1871, p. 248).*

Fig. a: suit for boy from 8 to 10 years old.
Fig. b: suit for boy from 5 to 7 years old.
Fig. c: suit for boy from 3 to 5 years old.
Fig. d: suit for boy from 3 to 5 years old.
Fig. e: suit for boy from 10 to 12 years old.
Fig. f: dress for girl from 12 to 14 years old.
Fig. g: suit for girl from 5 to 7 years old.

APRONS *(8.12.1871, p. 504).*
Fig. a: cambric apron.
Fig. b: linen apron.
Fig. c: apron with ruffles.

Fig. d: apron with ruche trimming.
Fig. e: apron with lace trimming.
Fig. f: apron with flounce set on.
Fig. g: gros grain apron with embroidery.

LADIES' SPRING AND SUMMER WRAP-PINGS *(5.6.1871, pp. 280–281).*
Fig. a: cashmere paletot, front.
Fig. b: half-fitting gros grain paletot, back.
Fig. c: cashmere paletot, back.
Fig. d: ladies'-cloth basque, back.
Fig. e: cashmere paletot, back.
Fig. f: paletot embroidered with chain stitch, back.

Fig. g: ladies'-cloth half-fitting paletot, back.
Fig. h: cashmere sacque, back.
Fig. i: half-fitting gros grain paletot, back.
Fig. j: violet barathea mantelet, back.
Fig. k: violet barathea mantelet, front.
Fig. l: light gray cashmere mantelet.

LADIES' AND CHILDREN'S SUMMER SUITS *(7.15.1871, pp. 440–441).*

Figs. a and b: suit for elderly lady, back and front.

Fig. c: foulard dress with high basque.

Fig. d: suit for girl from 2 to 4 years old.

Fig. e: suit for boy from 4 to 6 years old.

Fig. f: Percale walking suit.

Fig. g: Swiss muslin dress with over-skirt and heart-shaped neck.

Fig. h: dress for girl from 4 to 6 years old.

Figs. i and j: suit for elderly lady, front and back.

Figs. k and l: walking suit for young girl, back and front.

Fig. m: nurse's suit.

Fig. n: infant's robe.

Figs. o and p: écru foulard dress with over-skirt and basque.

Fig. q: dress with over-skirt and square-necked basque.

Fig. r: dress for girl under 2 years old.

Figs. s and t: piqué walking suit.

k   j   l   m   n   o   p

a   *b*   *c*   *d*

LADIES' AND CHILDREN'S BATHING COSTUMES *(8.19.1871, p. 521).* **Fig. a:** blue flannel suit, trimmed with white braid, consisting of wide trowsers and short over dress open in revers at the front. Gray cotton duck slippers with cord soles. **Fig. b:** child's bathing suit of light gray serge, trimmed with worsted braid. **Fig. c:** red flannel swimming or bathing costume, consisting of long trowsers closed above the ankles and high over dress trimmed with black braid. Black belt ribbon. Red trimmed hood. **Fig. d:** gray flannel swimming or bathing suit. Trowsers are wide and rather short; the over dress is closed to the neck. Long white flannel bathing mantle with hood. The hair is tied back with red ribbon. Manilla slippers.

OPERA TOILETTE *(12.2.1871, p. 760).* This picturesque toilette, from a new Paris model, is very effective at the opera or concert, and combines the three colors now so much in vogue. The under-skirt is of *ciel* blue faille, trimmed with a gathered flounce, which is surmounted by a bias fold and pleating. Princesse over dress of apricot faille, trimmed with ruches of *ciel* blue faille, and edged with lace round the neck. Half-flowing sleeves of apricot faille, slashed and underlaid with puffings of white silk, and trimmed blue faille ruches. Bodice of white silk, forming a square neck with the over dress, and trimmed with ruches of blue faille and lace. The over dress is looped much higher on the left side than the right by means of ruches. Blue silk slippers. Blue enamel and gold jewelery. Hair roped with pearls.

COSTUMES AND LINGERIE *(1.20.1872, p. 49).*
Fig. a: low-necked pointed basque-waist.
Fig. b: pink silk low-necked waist.

Fig. c: crinoline tournure.
Fig. d: cambric petticoat with train.
Fig. e: jaconet petticoat with train.
Fig. f: gray poplin dress, front.

Fig. g: brown velvet jacket, front.
Fig. h: brown velvet jacket, back.
Fig. i: gray poplin dress, back.

EVENING TOILETTE (*1.6.1872, p. 13*). This exquisite vaporous evening dress is made of white tulle and Malines lace, trimmed with zinnias of rich, bright colors, with dark leaves, which have the effect of the warm tints of autumn leaves, and produce a striking effect among the clouds of tulle. The trained skirt is puffed all the way to the waist, and trimmed with a deep flounce. The over-skirt is of plain tulle, edged with Malines lace headed with a pouf, and is cought up with zinnias so as to form diamond puffs. A long trailing spray of dahlias loops it at one side. Low puffed waist, edged round the neck with zinnias, and short sleeves. A coronet of the same flowers encircles the head, and a single zinnia is set on the crown. Necklace of gold pendants. White kid gloves and slippers.

EVENING TOILETTE *(3.9.1872, p. 180).* This rich and strikingly picturesque toilette has a petticoat of white silk, with a white lace flounce on the bottom, over which is worn a trained skirt of gold-colored satin, edged with a lavender ruche, with wide revers on each side the front breadth, faced with lavender satin, and edged with lavender ruches, and turned back so as to show the whole silk petticoat. Over-skirt of puffed lavender satin, edged with rich fringe of the same color, with revers on the side like those of the under-skirt, faced with gold-colored satin and ruches. Long trailing sprays of dark purple and gold pansies with green leaves cover the satin petticoat displayed by the revers at the sides. The low-necked lavender satin waist is cut in one piece with the over-skirt, and finished on the top with a bertha of gold-colored satin, simulating a revers, and covered with pansies like those on the skirt. Similar pansies are gracefully arranged on the puffed over-skirt. Short sleeves of lavender satin, with revers of gold-colored satin, separated by a single pansy. Marie Stuart frills of lace. Emerald and gold jewelry. Coiffure of purple and gold pansies. Lavender satin slippers. White kid gloves.

DOLLY VARDEN WALKING SUIT *(3.16.1872, cover).* This pretty Dolly Varden walking suit, front and back views of which are given in our illustration, is copied from the newest and most approved model of this favorite costume. In the first figure of the illustration, giving a front view, the Dolly Varden polonaise is made of flowered cretonne with a black ground, and is edged with a ruffle of the material four inches wide, headed by a band of black cretonne stitched on. The band and ruffle, graduated in size, extend up the waist, over the shoulders, and across the back. The Dolly Varden polonaise is worn over a skirt of black gros grain, trimmed on the bottom with a wide kilt pleating, surmounted by three rows of black silk braiding and black ribbon bows. In the second figure, which shows the side and back of the dress, the Dolly Varden polonaise is made of green foulard sprigged with bright flowers. It is edged with a ruffle of the material, set on with a heading, which is separated from the ruffle by tabs of green foulard, pointed at one end and overlapping each other, each tab being secured by a star-shaped silver button. The waist is closed with similar buttons, and is trimmed with the tabs and buttons, without the ruffles. The skirt is made of solid green foulard.

a   *b*   *c*   *d* *e*   *f*

**CONFIRMATION AND FIRST COMMU-
NION DRESSES** *(4.6.1872, p. 245).*
Fig. a: confirmation dress.
Fig. b: violet gros grain dress.

Fig. c: first Communion dress.
Fig. d: first Communion dress.
Fig. e: black poult de soie dress.
Fig. f: confirmation dress.

LADY'S VISITING TOILETTE *(6.8.1872, cover).* This elegant visiting costume has a trained skirt of violet silk, trimmed with four scalloped flounces, each surmounted by a band of black velvet ribbon. The over-skirt and waist are of a lighter shade of violet faille, trimmed with white lace and black velvet ribbon and bows. The waist, which is cut in one piece with a deep skirt, resembling a polonaise, is finished in the back with a hanging scarf of silk pleated lengthwise, and trimmed with white lace and velvet bows. Coat sleeves, worn under hanging sleeves, trimmed to correspond with the trimming of the back. Parasol of the same shade of violet as the over-skirt, edged with white lace. White chip bonnet, trimmed with light violet ribbon and yellow and purple pansies.

ORNAMENTS (7.20.1872, p. 477).
Fig. a: black velvet necklace with steel
   spangles.
Fig. b: salmon gros grain, black velvet and
   black lace bow for the hair.
Fig. c: rose-colored gros grain and black
   velvet bow for the hair.
Fig. d: green gros grain, black velvet and
   black lace bow for the hair.
Fig. e: lilac gros grain and black velvet bow
   for the hair.
Fig. f: crêpe de chine, lace and velvet bow
   for the hair.

SUMMER HATS AND BONNETS FOR YOUNG AND OLD LADIES *(8.3.1872, p. 509).*

Fig. a: maize crape hat.

Fig. b: gray crape bonnet for elderly lady.

Fig. c: white English straw hat.

Fig. d: white organdy garden hat with spray of flowers.

Fig. e: figured white and lilac batiste garden hat.

WATERING-PLACE TOILETTE (*8.17.1872, p. 545*). Walking Suit. This striking toilette is an early indication of fall costumes. Skirt of dark reddish-bronze silk trimmed with a kilt pleating set on in curves, and surmounted by two gathered flounces separated by three rather wide bias folds. Over-skirt of very pale pearl gray cashmere, closed in front with black buttons. The front of the over-skirt is edged with kilt pleating of the material, headed with cord. A long leaf-shaped tab on each side of the over-skirt extends far below the front. A large bow, with ends of silk like the under-skirt, scalloped on the edge and trimmed with two rows of cord, finishes the tab. The back of the over-skirt forms a large pouf. Basque of the same material as the over-skirt, edged with an embroidered strip, and furnished with wide brown silk scalloped revers, which are closed with buttons and button-holes. Hat of pale gray silk, trimmed with a feather and ribbons of the same shade. Brown boots of the color of the under-skirt.

WATERING-PLACE TOILETTE *(8.17.1872, p. 545)*. Evening dress. Trained skirt of *lilas-ancien* silk, richly embroidered with silk of the same tint, and trimmed on the sides from waist to bottom with seven gathered ruffles of a deeper tint, with a scalloped edge and embroidered heading of the first shade. Two broad ribbons of the deeper tint, edged with a lighter ruffle, pass from the side trimmings, and are tied in the back of the skirt, forming a pouf. The Pompadour waist and short tablier edged with white lace are of the deeper tint, as is also the upper part of the flowing sleeve. The lower part of the sleeve is also of the lighter silk, and is trimmed with a band and bow of the deeper shade. Straw-colored gloves. Gold necklace, medallion and earrings. Hair bow of the lighter shade of lilac.

BUSTLES, NIGHTWEAR AND WRAPPER
(9.21.1872, pp. 624–625).
Fig. a: muslin night-cap.
Fig. b: crinoline bustle.
Fig. c: dimity and steel-spring bustle.
Fig. d: lawn night-cap with tucks and em-
broidery.
Fig. e: lady's buff linen wrapper, back.
Fig. f: muslin night sacque with flowing
sleeves.
Fig. g: lady's buff linen wrapper, front.

LADY'S CARRIAGE DRESS *(9.14.1872, p. 612).* Skirt of striped purple and white silk, trimmed on the bottom with a gathered bias flounce, surmounted by a broad straight lengthwise band of the material, edged on each side by a narrow pleated ruffle. Basque-waist of the same material. Redingote with wide sleeves of white cashmere, trimmed with black velvet and passementerie. White straw bonnet, with purple revers, trimmed with purple and white ribbon and feathers, a white aigrette, and bright autumn leaves. Purple parasol, edged with white lace. Purple gloves.

a

b

c

d

e

WRAPS *(11.9.1872, p. 736).* The composite garments announced by Madame Raymond are found in great variety among the importations. They are combinations of the sacque and mantle arranged in fanciful ways; sometimes the back of the garment is a pointed cape, while the front is a regular sacque, and again there are postillion and sacque backs with graceful mantilla fronts. The new garment of which most is seen and heard is the Dolman. There are varieties of this wrap, but its peculiar feature is its great wing-like sleeve, or a side piece over the arm hanging in a point below the rest of the garment. **Fig. a:** black velvet mantle, back. **Fig. b:** black velvet mantle, front. **Fig. c:** braided cashmere Dolman, back. **Fig. d:** braided cashmere Dolman, front. **Fig. e:** steel blue cloth paletot.

LADY'S WALKING DRESS *(10.12.1872, p. 676)*. This pretty costume has a skirt of black faille, trimmed with a kilt-pleated flounce, surmounted with two rows of narrow puffing. Polonaise of bronze faille, with heart-shaped neck and Dolman sleeves, puffed on the top, the puffs being separated by narrow black velvet bands, embroidered in bright colors, and finished at the ends with black velvet bows. Over the waist of the polonaise are worn black velvet bretelles and braces, with tabs in the back, embroidered in silk with bright-colored flowers. Bronze silk hat, trimmed with coral ribbon and flowers. Bronze staff parasol. Bronze gloves.

EVENING TOILETTE (*1.25.1873, p. 60*). This graceful toilette for a full-dress reception is of salmon-colored faille. The demi-trained skirt, without flounces or over-skirt, has an elaborate trimming of white chenille balls, imitating pearls. The low square corsage is edged with point lace, and has lace frills across the back and front; also swinging chains of balls fall from the shoulders. The necklace and coiffure are also of chenille. Coral jewelry, set in massive Etruscan gold. Pink and yellow roses in the hair. Bouquet of violets and tearoses.

EVENING TOILETTE *(1.25.1873, p. 60)*. Evening dress of rose-colored faille, with untrimmed demi-train, and chatelaine bodice extending below the waist in the antique fashion. The over-skirt is of Valenciennes lace in quaint medieval design. The sash is of faille ribbon the color of the dress. The Grecian bertha is formed of this ribbon and lace. A lace frill surrounds the chatelaine bodice. Necklace and ear-rings of diamonds and red gold. Provence roses in the corsage and coiffure. Long kid gloves without buttons.

f   *g*

SKATING SUITS FOR MISSES AND YOUTHS FROM 4 TO 15 YEARS OLD *(1.25.1873, p. 56).*
Fig. a: suit for girl from 5 to 7 years old.
Fig. b: suit for girl from 4 to 6 years old.
Fig. c: suit for girl from 9 to 11 years old.
Fig. d: suit for girl from 11 to 13 years old.
Fig. e: suit for girl from 13 to 15 years old.
Fig. f: suit for boy from 9 to 11 years old.
Fig. g: suit for boy from 10 to 12 years old.

WATERING-PLACE COSTUME *(6.28.1873, p. 408).* This pretty costume is designed for visiting in country-houses, at watering-places, or for out-of-door fêtes, lawn-parties, and other summer festivals. The skirt is white muslin, puffed on the upper part of the front breadth, with flounces extending all around the skirt. The Pompadour polonaise with vest front is of rose-colored foulard, showing a pale blue lining on the side, and trimmed with a ruffle of rose-color, headed by a band of pale blue silk. The puffed muslin sleeves have blue silk bands latticed between the puffs, and rosettes of rose-color; blue bands and pink rosettes are also on the skirt. Chip Spanish gypsy, trimmed with rose and blue ribbons, and a bouquet of forget-me-nots and roses with brown foliage. Rose-colored foulard parasol, with blue bow and bamboo stick. Linen collar. Tortoise-shell jewelry. Pale blue gloves.

YOUNG LADY'S SPRING SUIT *(6.7.1873, p. 364)*. This costume of pearl gray foulard is designed for a young lady. The three front breadths are formed of kilt pleats, and have a straight side sash edged with a gray-blue band and yak lace. The back breadths are covered with lapping flounces. Apron over-skirt with wide straight sashes; a narrow bias gray-blue band and yak lace edge the upper skirt and sashes. Round Josephine waist with wide belt. Half-flowing sleeves and reversed cuffs. Mantle of gray-blue cashmere with hood. Straw hat, with straw flowers on the brim, standing loops of blue ribbon resting against the crown, and a pompom with scarlet tips.

RECEPTION DRESS *(7.5.1873, p. 428).* This elegant toilette, which is designed to be worn at day receptions, consists of a white silk petticoat, puffed lengthwise in front, and an over-dress of mauve silk, open in front, with a train of medium length. The skirt of the over-dress is edged with two ruffles, turned in opposite directions, and separated by a bias fold. A wide upright frill of mauve silk encircles the neck, and a pleated sash forms a pouf at the back of the skirt. White silk hat, trimmed with violet feathers and ribbon, and bound with black velvet ribbon, a long end of which falls behind. Mauve silk parasol.

CARRIAGE DRESS *(7.5.1873, p. 428)*. White muslin skirt, trimmed with four flounces, and ornamented in front with a trellis of violet ribbon. Over dress of leaf brown foulard, edged with violet ribbon, with revers at the side faced with violet silk. The sleeves of the over dress are short, with undersleeves of puffed white muslin, and violet ribbon trimmings. Leaf brown bonnet, with violet ribbon and pink roses. Leaf brown silk parasol.

a   b   c   d

LADIES' RIDING-HABITS *(7.5.1873, p.425).*
Fig. a: mohair riding-habit, front.
Fig. b: mohair riding-habit, back.
Fig. c: cloth riding-habit, back.
Fig. d: cloth riding-habit, front.

EVENING DRESS *(9.20.1873, p. 605).* This full-dress evening toilette is of groseille, or currant red faille, with an over-skirt of white Chambéry gauze. The demi-train skirt is of silk, with a Spanish flounce. The gauze over-skirt has a pleating on the edge, and is caught to the silk in horizontal puffs by garlands of variegated roses, red, pink, and yellow, with embrowned leaves. These garlands surround the whole skirt, except on the sides where the upper skirt is opened and forms medallions edged with a black lace ruche. The low round Josephine waist of silk has puffed gauze sleeves, and roses on the neck and bust. Roses are above the high puffed coiffure. The front of the hair is parted in the middle, and waved on the forehead. Pearl ear-rings, and necklace with ruby medallion. Wide gold bracelets, and a large Trianon fan.

EVENING TOILETTE *(11.8.1873, p. 716).* This tasteful evening dress is of black Chambéry gauze with gold-colored stripes, made over black silk. The skirt has the new fan train (just introduced by Worth), with a triple pleat in the lower part of the back breadth.

The stripes on the front breadth are arranged diagonally. The apron over-skirt is very long, and trimmed up the sides to the tournure. Round Josephine waist with square neck—a favorite style for new evening dresses. The trimming is the new appliqué embroidery of

silk and chenille on tulle, and represents scarlet, yellow, and black roses. The flowers of the corsage and in the hair are artificial. Belt and long loops of scarlet ribbon. Heavy gold jewelry.

CUIRASS POLONAISE WALKING SUIT *(10.24.1874, cover)*. This handsome and comfortable winter polonaise is copied from a Paris model, kindly furnished us by Messrs. Arnold, Constable, & Co. It is a new modification of the popular cuirass, and is designed to produce the effect of a close-fitting inflexible suit of armor. This result if obtained by trimming the waist and sleeves of the garment, which is of black camel's-hair, with rows of black Titan braid, which are arranged diagonally on the front of the waist, meeting herringbone fashion, and horizontally on the sleeves and back. The polonaise fits smoothly over the waist and hips, as if moulded to the figure. A row of black marten fur trimming, interspersed with white hairs, simulates a basque, and edges the bottom and neck of the garment. The polonaise is also trimmed on the bottom with ten horizontal rows of Titan braid, and is slightly draped. It is worn over a black silk walking skirt, trimmed in front with lengthwise puffs, and in the back with flounces.

VISITING TOILETTE *(12.27.1873, p. 828).* This elegant toilette for visiting is composed of plum-colored velvet and silk, with a border of otter fur. The short silk skirt has a deep box-pleated velvet flounce, showing a facing of silk at the top. The over-skirt of silk has a short wrinkled apron front and ample train with otter border. The long basquine has a pleated back, Dolman sleeves, and fur trimming. Plum velvet Normandy bonnet, with an ostrich ruche inside, and small yellow lilies. Buff kid gloves.

WORTH BASQUE AND FULL-TRAINED TRIMMED SKIRT *(12.19.1874, cover).* This elegant house, dinner, visiting, and evening dress is copied from a stylish toilette made by the celebrated Paris dress-maker, Worth, and furnished us by the kindness of Messrs. Lord & Taylor. The original dress is of black silk, richly trimmed with velvet, silk, and fringe. The basque, which is remarkably handsome, and forms a desirable variety from the plain cuirass, may be advantageously combined with a demi-trained or walking skirt for street wear, or plainer costumes. The full-trained skirt is cut in a new and admirable fashion, which combines gracefulness of effect with great economy of material. It is trimmed with a drapery formed of wings of unequal length, which take the place of an over-skirt.

II

NATURAL FORM AND CUIRASS BODY

❧ 1875-1882 ❧

"The ideal at present is the greatest possible flatness and straightness: a woman is a pencil covered with raiment" (October 23, 1875). It was, however, several years before the bustle was completely abandoned. When this ideal was achieved, to maintain flatness and straightness—and to provide variety in the "raiment" —asymmetry was introduced (Street Costumes, pp. 96, 102). Along with asymmetry came a variety of new approaches to both trimming and draping. To add to verticality, outerwear became nearly or entirely full-length, and was weighted down with fur, chenille fringes and braid passementerie applied in the manner of Eastern European and Siberian costumes (Lady's Ulster, p. 105; Ladies' Winter Wrappings, pp. 112-113). The slenderizing of the body continued downward, and by 1881 the knees had become so constricted by inner ties and construction that walking was reduced to small, mincing steps (Ball Toilette, p. 138; Spring Costumes, p. 140). The thighs were outlined and the hips returned to prominence, gradually growing to become the focal point and presaging the return of the bustle in the middle of the 1880s (Autumn and Winter Toilettes, p. 145).

Elaborate hairstyles were festooned with ornaments and false hairpieces (Ladies' Coiffures, pp. 81, 84; Hair Ornaments, p. 121). Complementing the diminishing roundness of the silhouette, hats grew impressive in shape and decoration. The Paris correspondent observed, "If dresses are simple, bonnets in revenge appertain more than ever to the domain of the fancy" (May 17, 1879).

The influence of the eighteenth century remained strong (Watering-place Toilette, p. 91; Dinner Toilette, p. 93; Promenade Costume, p. 98; Spring Costumes, p. 139; Watteau Wrapper, p. 141). In 1876, when America celebrated its Centennial, special gowns designed for various balls could do little more to reflect the spirit of 1776 (Toilettes at the Centennial, p. 100). Daytime apparel, however, by drawing from men's fashions of the eighteenth century, managed to convey some historic feeling ("Seventy-six" Walking Suit, p. 86; Glove-fitting Basque, p. 99). Since this was only a commemoration with little real significance, the effects were minor and relegated chiefly to details.

Fashion history is dotted with occasional fads. They flare up suddenly, shine for a short time, and then disappear completely. In 1875 dresses developed elaborate pockets (Visiting Costume, p. 78). They became so popular that to be consistent with the new asymmetrical design of the costumes, they survived as a single pocket placed so low and so far back that they were rendered impractical and were reduced to pure decoration (Reception Toilette, p. 88; Walking Suits, pp. 90, 110). Although many dresses were made with these pockets for two years, there is no sign of their use afterwards. The tennis apron was also short-lived (Lawn Tennis Aprons, p. 128).

There was great concern with the "natural form" during this cycle. While the fashionable version remolded the soft natural curves of the body into hard, rigid arcs (Full-dress Toilette, p. 103; Midwinter Toilettes, pp. 114–115), there was, at the same time, an Aesthetic movement in dress, similar to the one in decorative arts, that favored the flowing lines of antiquity and the middle ages. Fashion columns extolled the virtues of this revolution in dress for its simplicity, comparative inexpensiveness and lasting quality. "Another plea in favor of this style is the privilege it gives—nay almost extorts—of omitting corsets from the list of necessities" (July 16, 1881). Yet for all the discussion, *Harper's Bazar* had few illustrations of this kind of dress. Those which appear seem to be misinterpretations of the Aesthetic movement (Aesthetic Dress, p. 129).

Largely ignoring the petition for sanity in dress, the fashion plates continued to show ladies encased in stoutly-boned, long-waisted "cuirasses" (Cuirass Basque, p. 80), and slender, princesse lined gowns ending in heavy trains laden with trimming (Sea-side Toilette, p. 106). Added to the new preference for heavier fabrics and darker colors, this gave the ladies the appearance of slowly gliding tree trunks (Winter Costumes, pp. 130–131; Outdoor Costumes for Women and Children, pp. 142–143).

VISITING COSTUME. *(10.23.1875, p. 688).* This elegant Parisian costume for visiting represents the fashionable arrangement of the princesse robe with court train. The corsage, basque, and tablier are cut in one—that is, without seams at the waist—and are composed of reversed pleats of strawberry satin held down by bands of black velvet. The flounce across the boot and the sleeves are also reversed pleats and bands. The court train of faille of a deeper shade has a long full shirred breadth in the middle, and plain short side breadths trimmed with two velvet bands and a flounce. A large and elegant pocket on the right side is covered with black lace and velvet bows. Cavour collar of linen, with white lace cravat. Black velvet bonnet, with a torsade and face trimming of strawberry faille and roses; a long white ostrich plume is posed low behind. Blonde hair worn in a low Greek coil. Écru kid gloves.

MARQUISE SACQUE WITH DOUBLE-BRESTED VEST, TRIMMED OVER-SKIRT, AND SHORT COURT TRAIN *(10.23.1875, p. 688).* This stylish winter costume shows the tasteful combination now in vogue, but may also be used for striped and figured mixtures, or for costumes that are entirely of one fabric. Its principal feature is the long marquise sacque, which will serve as a model for ample winter wraps of cloth, cashmere, gros grain, or velvet. This sacque is long and loose in front, and slopes away to show a double-breasted vest. The vest is attached to the edge of the front, and is nearly close-fitted by stylish long side bodies, beginning in the shoulder seams. Pockets are placed on the back. The sleeves of the garment represented are fancifully trimmed, but they may be quite plain if preferred. The tablier consists of many diagonal puffs of the plaid goods sewed on a lower skirt of plain material. The pleated flounce, with puffed headings, is alike all around the bottom of the skirt. The short square-cornered court train is of straight breadths of the plain goods, caught up by sash loops of the plaid.

CUIRASS BASQUE, LONG SQUARE OVER-SKIRT, AND WALKING SKIRT *(10.23.1875, cover)*. This handsome suit includes the latest style of the favorite cuirass basque, which is more than ever in favor, and which is certain to continue the leading basque of the fall and winter. This, with the long square over-skirt, forms the popular over dress for woolen and silk costumes, and also for plain alpaca and merino dresses. They are of simple shape, easily made, and are becoming to all figures. The cuirass basque has the long stylish side bodies, with seams beginning on the shoulders instead of in the armholes; there is also a seam down the middle of the back. The long square over-skirt clings to the figure in front, and is made rather bouffant by a puff that is set in between the shirred upper parts of the back breadths. The bottom of the skirt is straight, the corners at the back are square, and a large sash bow conceals the end of the puff. This is an excellent model for black cashmere over dresses with silk lower skirts. In such cases the puff and bow are of silk. Plain silk costumes are also made by this pattern. In the original the skirt is of black silk, and the over-skirt and cuirass basque of black cashmere ornamented with silk embroidery.

LADIES' COIFFURES *(2.12.1876, pp. 104–105).*

a   b   c   d   e

LADIES' BALL AND EVENING DRESSES
(2.12.1876, pp. 104–105).
Fig. a: white cashmere sortie de bal.
Fig. b: white tulle and green poult de soie
   dress.
Fig. c: cream tarlatan and faille ball dress.
Fig. d: gray silk evening dress.

f　　　　g　　　　　　　　　h　　　　i

Fig. e: cream and prune silk gauze and gros
grain ball dress.
Fig. f: blue poult de soie ball dress.
Fig. g: pink tarlatan ball dress.
Fig. h: white crape ball dress.
Fig. i: blue silk ball dress.

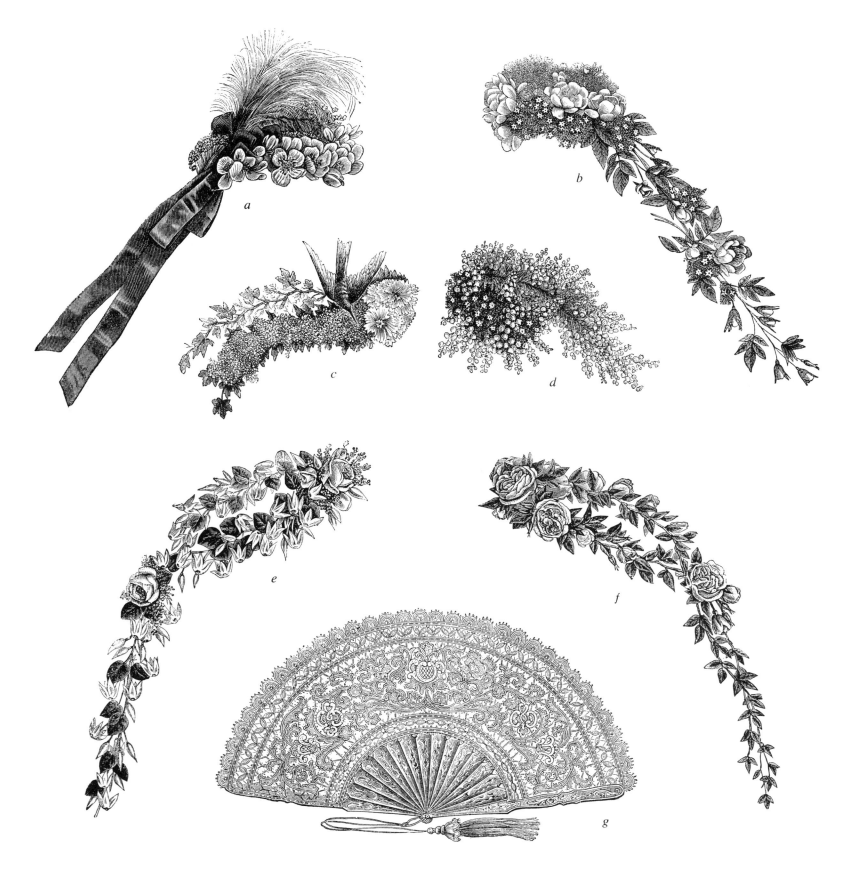

BALL AND EVENING COIFFURES *(2.19. 1876, p. 121).* **Fig. a:** one-half of this wreath is of jasmine flowers, and the other half is composed of forget-me-nots. In the back the wreath is finished with loops and ends of pale blue gros grain ribbon and heron feathers of the same color. **Fig. b:** trailing spray of similar flowers and rose leaves falls from the wreath down the nape of the neck. **Fig. c:** this wreath is arranged of brownish leaves, gilt grasses and pink carnations. A changeable bird completes the coiffure. **Fig. d:** this wreath is composed of a bunch of lilies-of-the-valley and slender grasses, from which a spray of similar flowers depends. **Fig. e:** this wreath with long trailing vine is composed of pink roses, heath, and Alpine violets and leaves. **Fig. f:** this wreath is arranged of pink roses, buds and leaves.

POINT LACE AND NEEDLE-WORK FAN. *(2.19.1876, p. 121).* **Fig. g.**

LADIES' WINTER HATS AND BONNETS *(2.19.1876, p. 121).* **Fig. a:** the wide brim of this white felt princess hat is turned up on the right side, and is furnished on the inside with a bandeau of red gros grain and an ostrich feather. A similar feather and cream-colored natte ribbon trim the crown of the hat. **Fig. b:** the brim of this gray felt bonnet is bound with black velvet and edged with steel galloon. The trimming consists of gray velvet and surah ribbon, gray wings, and pink roses. **Fig. c:** the brim of this black felt bonnet is bound with black velvet, and edged with silver galloon. On the inside the bonnet is trimmed with loops of velvet and cream-colored gros grain and with a humming-bird. Bows of velvet and gros grain and an ostrich feather trim the crown. **Fig. d:** the brim of this brown felt hat is turned up in the back. The trimming consists of velvet ribbon, ostrich feathers, a changeable bird, and heath. **Fig. e:** this black surah bonnet is trimmed in front with Chantilly lace and a rose with leaves. The crown is trimmed with flowers and bows of white surah fringed out on the ends. **Fig. f:** this blue surah bonnet has a white crown, and is trimmed on the brim with satin in a darker shade. Bows of similar satin, feathers, and roses form the trimming. Ribbons of surah, trimmed with black lace and tied under the chin, serve to keep the bonnet in place.

"SEVENTY-SIX" POLONAISE WALKING SUIT (*5.13.1876, cover*). This elegant and useful suit is copied from a beautiful Paris costume just imported, and furnished us by the courtesy of the distinguished modiste, Mrs. Connelly. It is well adapted to materials of all kinds, and may be simply or elaborately trimmed, according to the taste of the wearer. In the original the polonaise is of cloth and the skirt of silk.

LADIES' AND CHILDREN'S BATHING SUITS *(7.15.1876, p. 461).*
Fig. a: serge dress and carriage-leather dressing cape.

Fig. b: bathing suit for girl 6 to 8 years old.
Fig. c: blue flannel bathing suit.
Fig. d: red flannel bathing suit.

a   *b*

WALKING AND RECEPTION TOILETTES
(5.13.1876, p. 317). **Fig. a:** reception toilette.
This stylish dress is of black faille. The trained
skirt is trimmed high up with alternate wide
and narrow gathered flounces, surmounted by
a ruche. The polonaise is in the princesse
shape, that is, in one piece in front; the back
separates about five inches below the waist,
and falls square on the sides, the intervening
space being filled in with large loops of faille

ribbon, which form a cascade of trimming.
The bottom of the polonaise, the sleeves, and
large double pockets are trimmed with several
rows of jet galloon, which also form a square
bertha on the waist. The front of the polonaise
is edged with fringe. **Fig. b:** walking toilette.
This pretty costume is of London-smoke,
figured camel's-hair, and plain silk of the same
color. The skirt is of silk, with a gathered
flounce of camel's-hair. The camel's-hair

over-skirt is trimmed with silk pleating and
looped on the right side; this over-skirt forms
three draperies behind, edged with woolen
grelot fringe, and held by a faille bow. Large
silk pockets with a ribbon bow trim the front
of the over-skirt. Basque waist of camel's-hair
and silk. Bonnet of silk to match the costume,
with pink flowers and blue and black feathers.

STREET TOILETTE *(5.13.1876, p. 317)*. This lovely toilette has a skirt of sapphire blue faille, with a tablier of ivory moyen-age damask. The front breadths are trimmed with a deep gathered flounce, headed with a deep puffing, with a fluted heading and ruffle below. Train or court mantle of sapphire Sicilienne, laid in large organ-pipe pleats, which give it the necessary fullness. The tablier is bordered with a wide bias fold of sapphire Sicilienne, carelessly fastened together under a large bow without ends. The Sicilienne pocket is laid in pleats, lined with ivory damask, and ornamented with a large bow of sapphire faille. Cuirass basque of sapphire faille, slashed with ivory damask, and closed with sapphire buttons. Belgian straw bonnet, trimmed with turquoise blue faille, coquilles of ivory ribbon, and a bunch of blue feathers in two shades.

LA BOITEUSE POLONAISE WALKING SUIT *(5.27.1876, cover).* This elegant costume may be made up in any kind of costumerial. In the original the skirt is made of dark Havana brown faille, trimmed with two fluted flounces. The polonaise, of light Havana brown Sicilienne, has a full skirt, gracefully slashed behind, one end being square and the other rounded, whence its name. The skirt of the polonaise is artistically draped in the back by a heavy silk cord, knotted in the Dominican style, as shown in the illustration. The polonaise which is buttoned straight down the front is trimmed on the side with small bows of Havana brown ribbon. A large pleated faille pocket, in the shape of a cornet, is set on the side, and is finished at the bottom with a knot of flowing loops and ends of faille ribbon. The polonaise is edged with tasseled silk fringe of the same shade as the Sicilienne. Capote bonnet, with soft crown, encircled by a scarf of surah silk with ends falling behind, and trimmed with pale tea-roses, tastefully mixed with knots of ribbon.

WATERING-PLACE TOILETTE (*7.22.1876, cover*). This elegant toilette for visiting and driving at the watering-places is composed of India silk of pale cream-color combined with dark gray faille. The gray demi-train is bordered with a knife-pleating that is held on by two rows of machine stitching. The over-skirt has a long double square tablier, showing the cream-colored India silk in the centre with gray faille coming under the sides; each tablier is edged around the bottom and up the sides with gray pleating and cream-colored cashmere lace. The back of the over-skirt is the India silk gracefully draped over the train. The Joan of Arc cuirass is of the India goods, trimmed to match the over-skirt. The sleeves are of gray faille, with cream-colored puffs down the centre; also, cuffs of the India silk edged with gray pleatings, and lace and ornamented with a gray bow. Around the shoulders of the cuirass is a peasant fichu of gray faille trimmed with lace and a frill of the gray silk, and finished by a long looped bow on the breast. The neck is cut in heart-shape, has a revers of gray silk and a ruche of crêpe lisse. Capote bonnet of cream-colored silk, with a ruche in front, and a wreath of artemisias, cream, rose, and pearl-color. India silk parasol of cream-color, with ivory stick. Long undressed kid gloves.

VISITING TOILETTE (8.19.1876, p. 541). This superb toilette is made of pearl gray faille, richly trimmed with bands of dark crimson and pearl gray velvet, and dark crimson cords and tassels. The trained skirt is bordered with two rows of velvet trimming and several rows of heavy crimson cord. The long over-skirt has a point behind, and is gracefully draped under a large rosette of the material, with the aid of cords and tassels, as shown by the illustration. The plain waist is laced behind and cut away at the sides, and is edged with the velvet trimming, which is carried over the right shoulder to simulate a scarf. The sleeves are close to just below the elbow, where they fall open in large, flowing points, and are finished with cords and tassels.

DINNER TOILETTE *(8.19.1876, p. 541)*. This elegant toilette is made of cream-colored faille with purple satin stripes and purple crêpe de Chine. The princesse dress is of striped faille, and is trimmed on the bottom with a bias flounce, slightly gathered and piped with plain faille. Above the flounce is a puffing of the striped material, finished on each side with a narrow ruffle piped with faille. Over-skirt of purple crêpe de Chine, square and long behind, and trimmed with heavy netted fringe. The over-skirt is formed of two broad scarves, which, beginning at the right and left side, cross in front, and are carried around the skirt to the back, where they are knotted, and fall over the train, and are finished with a large crêpe de Chine bow with fringed ends. The corsage is cut square in front and is laced in the back, and is trimmed with Boiteuse drapery, which, beginning on the left shoulder where it is held by a crêpe de Chine bow, passes round the neck and across the right shoulder diagonally to the left side of the waist, where it is fastened under another bow of crêpe de Chine. Marie Antoinette sleeves with a wide pleating at the bottom, and a scarf of crêpe de Chine with a bow on the arm. Pleated gauze collar and undersleeves. This picturesque toilette is also very effective when made of muslin or foulard with blonde trimming.

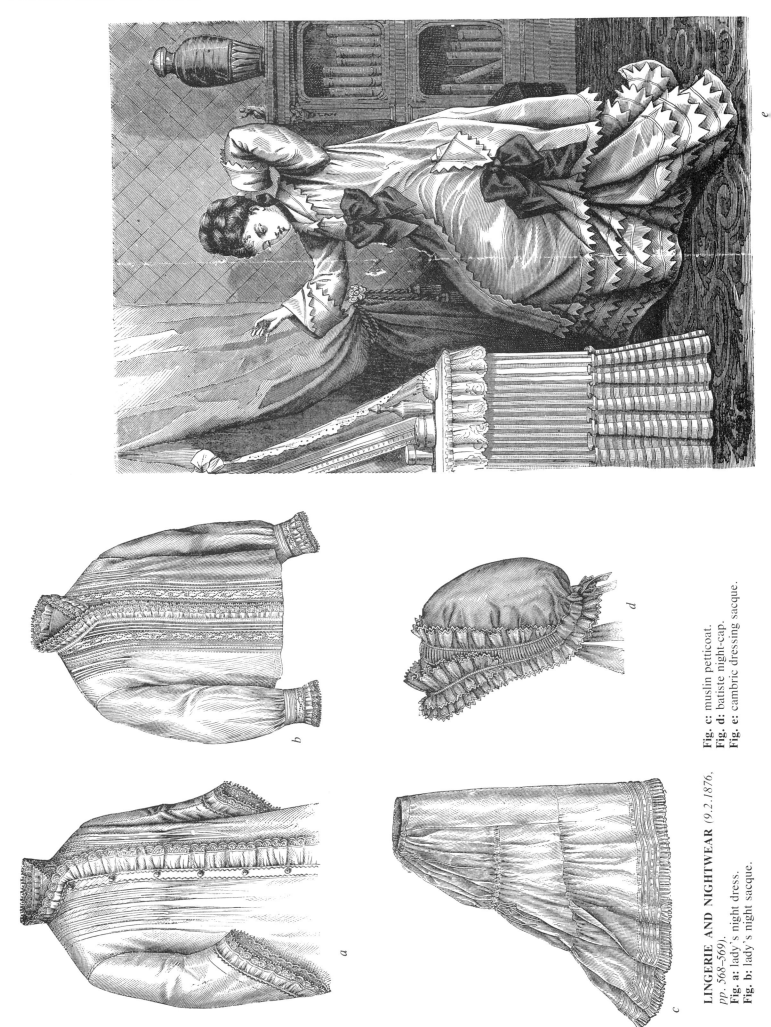

LINGERIE AND NIGHTWEAR *(9.2.1876, pp. 568–569).*
Fig. a: lady's night dress.
Fig. b: lady's night sacque.
Fig. c: muslin petticoat.
Fig. d: batiste night-cap.
Fig. e: cambric dressing sacque.

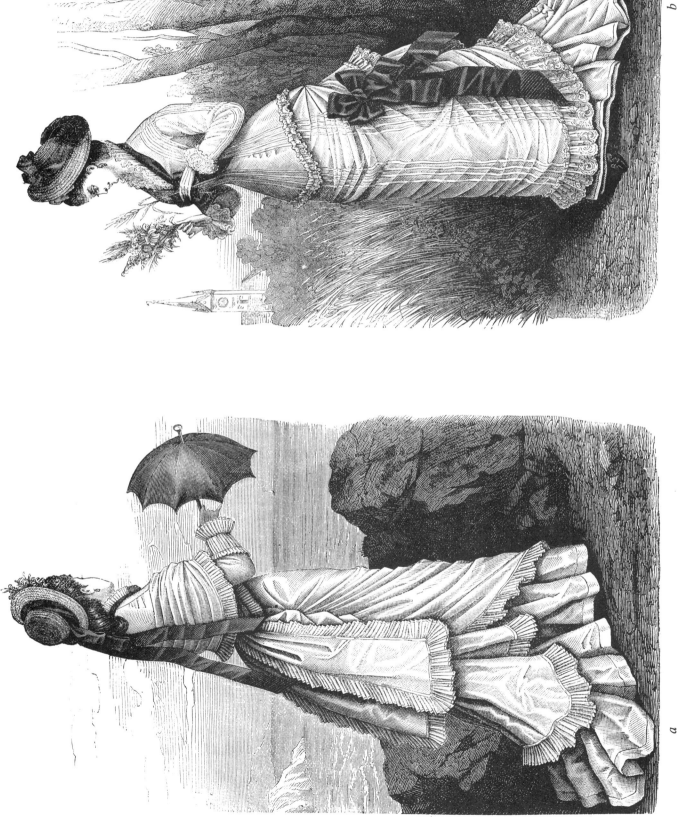

a

b

WHITE VICTORIA LAWN AND NANSOOK SUITS *(9.2.1876, cover).* **Fig. a:** The skirt of this white Victoria lawn suit is trimmed with a deep flounce furnished with a hem two inches wide at the bottom. The trimming for the over-skirt, sleeves, and scarf consists of side-pleated lawn ruffles. For the scarf a piece of lawn three yards and three-eighths long and three-quarters of a yard wide is required. Side-pleated ruffles trim the middle of the scarf on the under edge and the ends all around. Brussels straw bonnet, trimmed with ruby serge ribbon and poppies. Red parasol. **Fig. b:** The skirt of this nansook suit is trimmed with a deep flounce, and the over-skirt and waist are run in narrow lengthwise tucks. Narrow and broad white lace and bows of black gros grain ribbon form the remainder of the trimming. Italian straw bonnet, trimmed with cream-colored serge ribbon and a black ostrich feather.

STREET COSTUME *(8.26.1876, p. 557)*. This handsome costume is made of navy blue faille and **Russian** gray camel's-hair, striped with light yellow and blue, and trimmed with fringe of these two colors to match. The faille skirt is trimmed with two bias flounces of striped camel's-hair, bound with yellow, and edged with a narrow pleating of faille; the upper flounce is surmounted by a puffing and pleated heading. The polonaise of striped camel's-hair is trimmed with rich fringe, and buttoned behind, on the side. The front of the polonaise is trimmed with a point of faille, bound with yellow, and forming a buttoned revers. The polonaise is draped in front, a little on the bias, and simulates a double tablier, terminating on the left side, under an unclasped buckle, so as to leave a little of the skirt uncovered. The second skirt is slightly draped behind, and falls gracefully in a rounded sash end. A square piece of faille, trimmed with three bows, and set on the back just above the draping, completes the polonaise. The waist of the polonaise is cut square in front, and trimmed with a pleating and gamp of faille. Faille sleeves, with striped cuffs, slashed on the top in the form of a chevron, and finished with a double row of buttons.

a

b

c

SUMMER BONNETS *(6.9.1877, p. 357).*
Fig. a: this bonnet has a high peaked crown
and a broad chip brim, turned down at the
left side, curving up in a revers on the right,
and laid in a box pleat in the back. The crown
is covered with pleated white gros grain, of
which the fan-shaped upright trimming in
front is also made. A bow of white satin ribbon
held with a filigree agrafe, and a spray of pink
roses, mignonette, and leaves, are set against
the fan-shaped trimming. A similar bow with
agrafe is set on the back of the bonnet above
the box pleat. A mandarin rose with leaves,
and long ends of white satin ribbon, are set
under the brim in the back. **Fig. b:** this Italian
straw bonnet has a broad brim turned up in
the back and front. The trimming is composed
of white ostrich feathers and white roses. Two
feathers and two roses trim the front, and a
third feather fastened with a bow of white
satin ribbon, falls over the brim. A fourth
feather, fastened to the brim in the back completes the novel arrangement. The white satin
ribbon proceeding from the sides of the bonnet
is tied in the back. Three white roses trim
the inside of the bonnet in front. **Fig. c:** the
broad brim of this Tuscan straw bonnet is
turned down in front and up on the sides.
The trimming consists of mandarin satin ribbon eight inches wide, which is tied in a knot
in front. A cluster of buttercups, heath blossoms, grasses and ferns is set on this knot.
On the back of the brim, which is turned up,
set an ivory crêpe lisse scarf bordered with
side-pleatings which are edged with lace. This
scarf is held by a broad filigree buckle. A
crêpe lisse ruche trims the inside of the
bonnet.

PROMENADE COSTUME *(9.9.1876, cover).* This elegeant costume is composed of the new dark cream-colored faille, with an over dress of cream and white striped India silk, trimmed with cardinal red bows and cream-colored lace. The foundation is a princesse dress of plain cream-colored faille, buttoned diagonally its whole length, and trimmed with three knife-pleatings and a flounce of the lace. The striped India silk over dress is attached to the left shoulder, crosses the front diagonally, and is draped on the right side under a coquille of lace, which also appears to hold the scarf or sash ends of cardinal red faille. A fichu on the chest is held in front by red roses. The sleeves are trimmed with rows of lace and large cardinal bows. White chip hat, with the turned-up brim filled in with a cluster of red roses. Cream-colored feathers fall over the front, and are held on the crown by cardinal loops. Red foulard parasol, lined with cream-colored silk, and bordered with lace like that of the costume.

GLOVE-FITTING BASQUE, LOWDRAPED OVER-SKIRT, AND WALKING SKIRT (*10.21.1876, cover*). This pretty suit comprises the most popular styles of the present season for ordinary street and house wear, and may be made up in any style of material, and trimmed according to the fancy of the wearer. The basque is moulded closely to the figure, with two side bodies and two darts, and is pointed in the front and back. The long clinging over-skirt is gracefully draped low down on the figure, in conformity with the prevailing fashion, and is very nearly as long as the walking skirt over which it is worn.

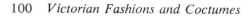

b

a

TOILETTES AT THE CENTENNIAL
(10.21.1876, p. 681). These beautiful dresses
have won universal admiration, and the
engravings of them may well serve to
illustrate, in future years, the fashions that
prevailed at the time of our first Centennial
anniversary. **Fig. a:** morning dress. This
beautiful morning dress is in Pompadour style
and colors, with pale blue silk in front and
as facings, white flowered brocade for the

robe, and pink bows for trimming. The plain
blue front is edged with two blue box-
pleatings, one of which extends around the
entire robe. The brocaded front is laid on the
blue, and edged with white appliqué lace,
beneath which are loops and ends of pink
ribbon. On the side is a long pocket of blue
silk held by pink bows. The sleeves are of
shirred blue silk, with over-sleeves of white
held by a pink bow at the elbow, and finished

below by organdy pleatings. The Watteau
back forms a graceful train, edged with lace
and pleated silk. Around the neck is a standing
pleating of lisse. **Fig. b:** exposition polonaise
and full-trained skirt. This elegant costume
has a polonaise of cream-colored damask
camel's-hair, with sleeves, skirt, and trimmings of myrtle green silk. The skirt is made
with a long train, and is trimmed with clusters
of pleatings. The polonaise is buttoned down

the entire front with green buttons, and has
a band of green silk and cream-colored fringe
on the edge. The back of the polonaise has
rich green passementerie, fringe, and double
loops of green silk. The green sleeves have
cream-colored cuffs. The collar is also of
green silk.

LADIES' AND CHILDREN'S SKATING SUITS *(12.2.1876, p. 781).*
Fig. a: gros grain and limousine suit.
Fig. b: camel's-hair suit.

Fig. c: silk suit.
Fig. d: faille and cashmere suit.
Fig. e: suit for boy from 6 to 8 years old.
Fig. f: suit for girl from 8 to 10 years old.

STREET SUIT *(12.2.1876, cover).* This stylish suit for the first cool days of winter is of striped camel's-hair of golden brown shades, trimmed with a bias band of silk of the same shade and with caroubier red braid, with woolen fringe of caroubier-color in a trellised pattern edged with balls. The skirt has no flounces, but a trimming of silk, braid, and fringe. The long princesse polonaise is buttoned down the entire front, has a Marguerite back, and is draped differently on the sides, the right side having a revers of silk, braid, and buttons. The trimming also outlines a yoke on the shoulders. The bonnet is felt, the color of the dress, trimmed with red berries, plumes, and loops of silk.

FULL-DRESS TOILETTE. *(12.9.1876, cover).* This elegant full-dress toilette illustrates several of the new features of such dresses, the square neck, as now worn, the princesse basque, with ends concealed under the scarf drapery, the diagonal tablier, the square train, the foliage embroidery, and lastly, the combination of three colors. In this instance the basque and tablier are of coral faille, the scarf and train of ivory Sicilienne, and the chenille passementerie is green foliage caught on the waist and train by red poppies. The basque buttoned in front has fan seams that make it fit as plainly as a corset. The square neck has a shoulder-strap that forms a sleeve and is edged with white lace. The

garland of leaves extends around the entire neck, and has two corsage bouquets posed in a way now in vogue. The coral faille skirt is very narrow, has two gathered flounces at the foot, and diagonal drapery in front, on which are three diagonal garlands of foliage.

The ivory white Sicilienne scarf is pleated around the figure, hides the edge of the basque, and its ends are hidden behind under the square court train, and held by a spray of red poppies. The long white train is embroidered all around with shaded olive green poppy leaves. Black velvet dog-collar with red gold pendant. Pompadour coiffure with a white heron's feather aigrette and one red poppy. Long white undressed kid gloves cut in the new shape without buttons at the wrist. Massive gold bands on the wrists.

a   b

BOY'S AND LADY'S RIDING SUITS
(12.9.1876, p. 796). **Fig. a:** riding suit for boy
from 10 to 12 years old. This suit of dark
brown cloth consists of trowsers, vest and
jacket, and is trimmed with rows of stitching
and buttons. Collar and cuffs of fine linen,
and felt hat. **Fig. b:** lady's riding-habit. The
princesse dress of black cloth is closed in front
with buttons and button-holes. On the left side
is a pocket. Collar and cuffs of fine linen.
Blue gros grain cravat. A blue gauze veil is
wound around the crown of the black beaver
hat.

LADY'S ULSTER WITH RUSSIAN HOOD *(12.9.1876, p. 797).* This convenient Ulster, for the model of which we are indebted to the courtesy of Messrs. Arnold, Constable, & Co., is the favorite pattern for water-proof cloaks, steamer or traveling cloaks, and linen dusters. The front is made double-breasted, the back is gracefully shaped, the sleeves are close, the hood is simply fashioned, and the whole garment is as light as it is possible to make so large a wrap. A cape is dispensed with in order to contribute to its lightness. English water-proof cloth in blue or gray shades is the favorite material.

SEA-SIDE TOILETTE *(8.11.1877, cover).* This striking picturesque toilette consists of a princesse dress of mandarin yellow silk, over which is worn a sleeveless polonaise of ivory white India cashmere. The skirt of the dress is simply trimmed with a closely gathered flounce, surmounted by a reversed heading, and supported by a *balayeuse* of white muslin, edged with Valenciennes. The polonaise, which is very clinging, and falls gracefully over the train, is bordered with black velvet ribbon, embroidered with shaded green, yellow ochre, and Egyptian red arabesques. The sleeves of the dress have black velvet cuffs, trimmed in a similar manner. The polonaise is laced in front with a white silk cord, and is drawn in around the hips by a heavy mandarin yellow cord and tassels. Both the dress waist and polonaise open low at the throat, and are furnished with a double turned-down collar, one of yellow silk and the other of white cashmere, under which a broad mandarin yellow ribbon is passed, and tied carelessly in a bow in front. White rice straw hat, with a high square crown and turned-up brim, under which is a wreath of shaded yellow roses. A *panache* of white feathers covers the crown in front, while a large white plume falls on the nape of the neck. A large rosette of mandarin yellow ribbon completes the trimming. Mandarin yellow parasol, lined with white, and finished on top with a cluster of yellow flowers.

SINGLE-BREASTED SQUARE COAT, FAN OVER-SKIRT, AND DEMI-FAN-TRAINED SKIRT *(12.23.1876, cover)*. This stylish Paris suit has a skirt of Havana brown faille, with an over-skirt and coat of camel's-hair of a lighter shade trimmed with blue fox fur. It is equally well suited to any other kind of material, and the coat may be used as an independent wrap, of beaver, basket-woven, or any other kind of cloth. In the model the skirt is trimmed with a wide knife-pleating stitched through the middle—the lower part being straight, and the upper part turned back so as to form shells. The long clinging over-skirt is looped on the sides, and falls thence in graceful folds on the fan train. The back breadth is slashed at the bottom, and fastened together with buttons and button-holes. The single-breasted coat is trimmed down the front with brandebourgs and passementerie loops or simulated button-holes, which also trim the pockets and deep cuffs. White felt bonnet, with high pointed crown and brim turned up at the side, trimmed with a light Havana brown feather and a faille puff of the darker shade, held by a steel buckle, and a large red rose with green leaves at the side.

a

b

c

d

e

f

g

h

CHATELAINE POCKET *(2.19.1876, p. 117).* **Fig. a:** this pocket is made of black velvet, and is furnished with a handle, belt hook, and chain of chased silver. The front of the pocket is ornamented with a coat of arms and a monogram worked in satin and half-polka stitch with silver thread.

SHOES, SLIPPERS AND BOOTS *(3.4.1876, p. 149).* **Fig. b:** this black patent-leather slipper is lined with white faille. The lining is ornamented with a cross seam of purple

silk. The high heel is covered with purple satin. On the middle of the front of the slipper is a bow composed of purple satin, arranged in fan shape, and of silver bullion, and to both sides of this bow is joined a leaf trimming of similar satin and silver bullion. **Fig. c:** this black kid slipper is furnished with a high heel covered with leather. The middle of the front is trimmed with a rosette of blue and black silk ribbon. **Fig. d:** this black kid shoe has a high heel covered with kid. From the front to the upper edge the shoe is furnished with

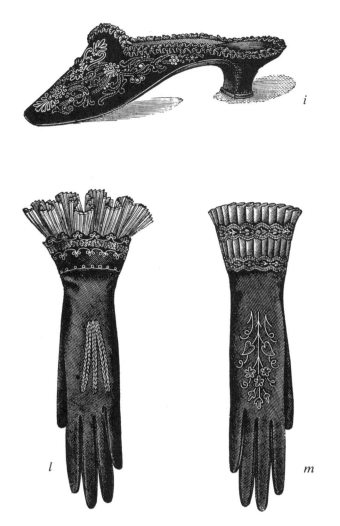

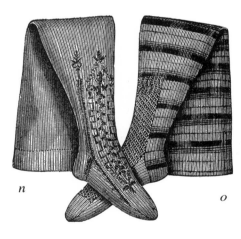

bands, which are bound with narrow black silk ribbon, and are furnished with button-holes in both ends. The buttons are set on the edge of the shoe as shown in the illustration. The middle of the front of the shoe is trimmed with a bow of narrow black silk ribbon. For evening toilettes the bands and buttons should be made of material to match the color of the dress. **Fig. e:** the lower part of this seal-skin and French kid boot, which is furnished with a double sole and high heel, is made of seal-skin bordered with a strip of yellow leather. The back is slashed on both sides to overlap the front, and is furnished with black silk ribbons, which are tied in a bow. The top of French kid is made to button; on the under-lapping part black buttons are fastened, and the over-lapping part is fur-nished with button-holes, and is scalloped on the outer edge and ornamented with stitching. **Fig. f:** this black kid boot has a high heel covered with leather. The sides are furnished with elastic. An ornamental piece of kid is stitched on the toe of the foot. The top but-toned on the boot is of kid lined with purple satin, and consists of two parts, which are closed with buttons. The overlapping front is scalloped and furnished with button-holes, and the corresponding buttons are set on the back. A rosette of black silk ribbon and lace trims the middle of the top.

TRAVELLING BAG (6.7.1877, p. 356).
Fig. g: travelling bag, closed.
Fig. h: travelling bag, open.

ACCESSORIES (7.7.1877, p. 356). **Fig. i:** the lady's slipper with Greek gold embroidery is worked on a foundation of brown velvet with gold and silver cord and is furnished with a heel covered with brown leather. **Fig. j:** this fraise with jabot is made on a rounded stiff foundation of pleated white Swiss muslin, side-pleated ruffles, and white and blue lace an inch wide. **Fig. k:** this fraise is edged at the top with box-pleated ruche of Swiss mus-lin and lace and with a ruche of Vulcan red gros grain ribbon. The jabot, which is sewn on the fraise is made of red and mandarin gros grain ribbon and is trimmed with lace. **Fig. l:** this glove of black Marseilles kid is embroidered in chain and half-polka stitch with tilleul floss silk, and is trimmed with a ruffle of side-pleated crêpe lisse laid in box pleats. **Fig. m:** this glove of black Marseilles kid is trimmed on the back of the hand with a spray-embroidered chain stitch with fine brown and yellow silk. A side-pleating of til-leul serge borders the under edge and forms the cuff. **Fig. n:** this stocking of fine écru thread is embroidered on the instep with filling silk of the same color in satin, black, and button-hole stitch, and in point Russe. This embroidery is intersected with single strips forming cross seams. **Fig. o:** this stocking of fine white cotton is interwoven with narrow red and wide brown stripes. On the instep is a design composed of diagonal open-work stripes of white cotton.

WALKING SUIT *(8.11.1877, p. 508).* This pretty suit consists of a skirt, polonaise, and long close-fitting jacket. The skirt is of claret faille, trimmed on the bottom with a deep side-pleated flounce, surmounted by a wide puff and narrow side-pleating. The polonaise of gray foulard is closed diagonally on the left side, and slightly looped at the bottom. The polonaise is trimmed on the bottom and up the side seams with a side-pleating, surmounted by a bias fold of claret faille. The gray foulard jacket is bordered with claret faille; the cuffs, collar, and pockets are of the same material. Tuscan straw bonnet, with scarf of claret faille wound around the crown, and bunches of thistles on the side and in front under the brim.

WATERING-PLACE TOILETTE *(8.11.1877, p. 508).* This handsome suit has a skirt of dark brown gros grain, trimmed on the bottom with two gathered flounces. The Breton polonaise of cream wool is trimmed with var- iegated galloon, with a red, blue, yellow, and white Persian pattern, and fringe of the same colors. The rolling collar is formed of the same galloon, which likewise trims the cuffs and the seams of the sleeves. The polonaise is slashed at the sides, and finished with bows of brown ribbon. Three rows of pearl buttons are set in front; the back is also ornamented with buttons. Tuscan straw hat, trimmed with brown ribbon, with a ruche inside the brim.

a   *b*   *c*   *d*   *e*

LADIES' WINTER WRAPPINGS *(11.17. 1877, p. 733)*.
Fig. a: Siberian cloak.
Fig. b: Serbian sacque.
Fig. c: Bulgarian sacque.
Fig. d: Roumanian cloak and walking skirt.
Fig. e: Toulouse cloak.
Fig. f: Plevna pelisse and walking skirt.
Fig. g: Masaniello sacque.

f   *g*

a   *b*

MIDWINTER TOILETTES *(1.31.1880, pp. 76–77).* **Fig. a:** this frained dress is of gray-blue faille and satin, trimmed with embossed velvet and fringe. The faille skirt is trained, and trimmed with a wide border of knife-pleatings in front, with only two pleatings behind. The over-skirt is composed of two satin scarf aprons edged with fringe, and has long graceful draping behind. The upper apron conceals the edge of the front and sides of the basque, and passes beneath the back. The basque has a vest of the velvet, with collar, cuffs, and revers of the same. **Fig. b:** this visiting dress has a basque of Oriental cashmere, with skirts of bronze satin. The demi-trained satin skirt has a pleated front cut out in vandykes that are trimmed with the cashmere, and fall over bands of the satin and knife-pleatings. The back has twisted scarf drapery. The basque opens over a satin vest. The bronze velvet hat has ostrich plumes of bronze

c   d

and dark red shades. Light bronze-colored gloves. **Fig. c:** this picturesque dress for the house is composed of soft gray India cashmere and garnet velvet. The skirt of cashmere has a plain flowing train, while the tablier is formed by two great puffs at the top, and has a knee scarf or sash knotted across it below. The garnet velvet corsage

fastens on one side underneath a puffed cashmere vest of Breton shape. A large collar of cashmere is trimmed with fringe. **Fig. d:** this graceful dress for carriage visiting is composed of amaranth-colored silk and wool goods with satin of the same shade. The trained skirt is laid in the lengthwise pleats, called *religieuse*. The princesse over-skirt

opens in front, drapes the back, and falls in a point nearly to the end of the train. The basque has a habit back, with a pleated satin belt in front. It has long ends in front, terminated by black satin bows. The fur border is silver-beaver. The bonnet is gray satin antique, trimmed with gray satin and ostrich plumes of two shades of gray.

l   *m*   *n*

CLOTHES FOR INFANTS AND CHILDREN
(6.12.1880, pp. 376–377).
Fig. a: dress for girl from 1 to 2 years old.
Fig. b: dress for girl from 3 to 5 years old.
Fig. c: dress for girl from 6 to 8 years old.
Fig. d: mousseline de laine dress.
Fig. e: dimity dress and piqué bib.
Fig. f: infant's piqué cloak and cashmere hood.
Fig. g: infant's batiste robe with blouse.
Fig. h: infant's nansook robe.
Fig. i: nurse's dress.
Fig. j: dress for girl from 4 to 6 years old.
Fig. k: infant's long petticoat.
Fig. l: foulard dress.
Fig. m: nurse's dress.
Fig. n: flannel diaper drawers.

SLIPPERS *(1.22.1881, p. 52).*
Fig. a: lady's ball slipper with Spanish embroidery.
Fig. b: lady's slipper.

BAGS *(3.5.1881, pp. 152–153).*
Fig. c: gros grain bag.
Fig. d: plush bag.

WHITE SATIN SLIPPER *(2.12.1881, p. 100).*
Fig. e.

BLUE VELVET SLIPPER *(10.15.1881, p. 660).* **Fig. f.**

BLUE SATIN SLIPPER *(7.23.1881, p. 469).* **Fig. g.**

SILVER BOUQUET-HOLDER *(10.8.1881, p. 653).* **Fig. h.**

FLORAL ORNAMENTS AND FANS *(12.17. 1881, p. 812).*

Fig. a: rose-bud and leaves.
Fig. b: knot of ribbons and evergreens.
Fig. c: knot of ribbons and evergreens.
Fig. d: corsage bouquet.
Fig. e: corsage bouquet.

Fig. f: black satin fan with chain stitch embroidery.
Fig. g: white satin fan with gold embroidery.
Fig. h: black satin fan with feather stitch embroidery.
Fig. i: old gold satin fan with feather border.

CONFIRMATION DRESSES *(4.2.1881, p. 221).*   **Fig. c:** figured organdy dress.
Fig. a: nuns' veiling dress.   **Fig. d:** batiste dress.
Fig. b: mull dress.

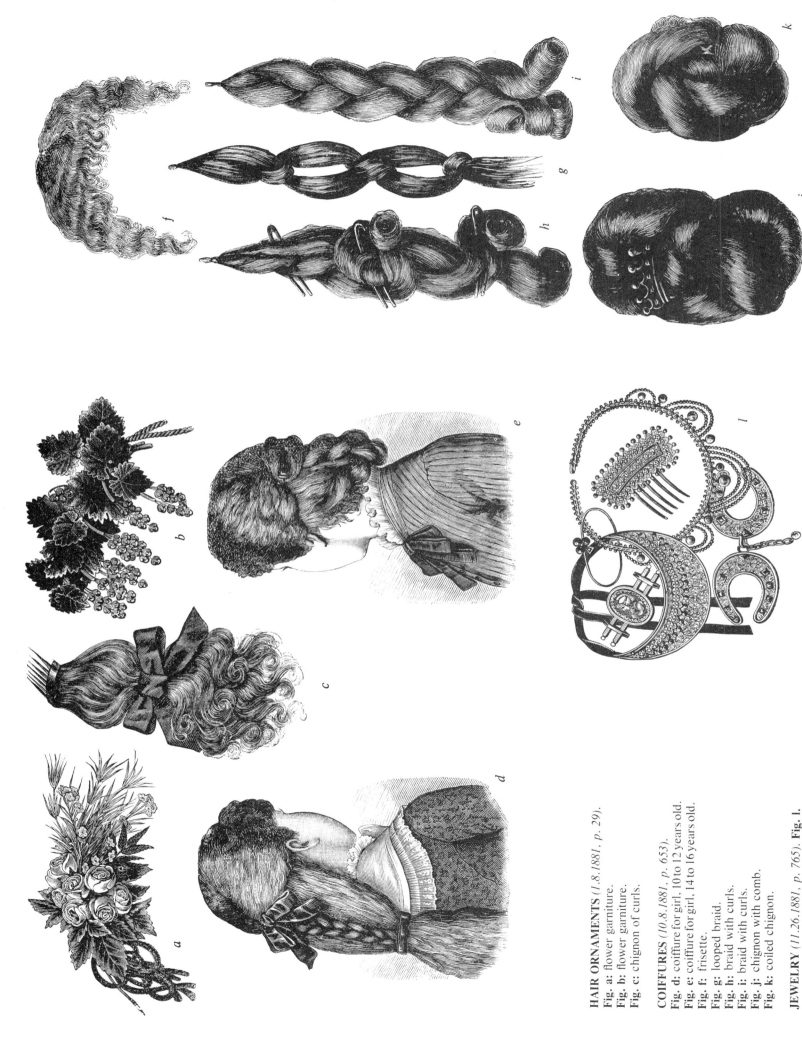

HAIR ORNAMENTS (*1.8.1881, p. 29*).
Fig. a: flower garniture.
Fig. b: flower garniture.
Fig. c: chignon of curls.

COIFFURES (*10.8.1881, p. 653*).
Fig. d: coiffure for girl, 10 to 12 years old.
Fig. e: coiffure for girl, 14 to 16 years old.
Fig. f: frisette.
Fig. g: looped braid.
Fig. h: braid with curls.
Fig. i: braid with curls.
Fig. j: chignon with comb.
Fig. k: coiled chignon.

JEWELRY (*11.26.1881, p. 765*). **Fig. l.**

DAMASSÉ SILK AND SATIN EVENING TOILETTE *(1.29.1881, p. 69).* This stylish toilette for full-dress occasions has a basque, long apron, and flowing train of Isabelle yellow brocaded satin, with darker golden brown plush laid in pleats beneath the apron front and under the train. The square neck of the basque has a full frill of white point duchesse lace. The sleeves are gracefully caught up inside the arm. A full pleated muslin balayeuse is used in the train instead of a separate trained petticoat. The fringe is of amber beads on crimped silk.

a   *b*

LADY'S AND CHILD'S SLEIGHING SUITS *(3.12.1881, cover).* **Fig. a:** this warm costume for a girl of eight years has a coat of drab lamb's-wool cloth, bordered with chinchilla fur. The cap is of chinchilla, and the muff also. **Fig. b:** this graceful surtout is of black Sicilienne, lined with squirrel-lock fur, and bordered with black lynx. The beaver bonnet is also black, trimmed with red ostrich plumes and shaded red ribbon. The dress is of black satin de Lyon combined with brocade. The skirt is trimmed with five side-pleated flounces.

a

b

POLONAISE   COSTUMES   *(6.4.1881,*
p. 357).
Fig. a: batiste polonaise and round skirt.
Fig. b: Medicis suit; hooded cape, polonaise
round skirt.

c

d

SUITS *(6.18.1881, p. 397).*
Fig. c: brown wool travelling suit; hooded
   cape, polonaise, round skirt.
Fig. d: country suit; hooded polonaise,
   round skirt.

d

e

b

c

a

f   *g*

BONNET, SLIPPERS AND BATHING COSTUMES *(7.2.1881, p. 429).*
Fig. a: Tuscan straw poke bonnet.
Fig. b: red flannel bathing suit and hat.
Fig. c: flannel bathing suit and hat.
Fig. d: ladies' crochet slipper.

Fig. e: Turkish travelling slipper.
Fig. f: Turkish towelling bathing cloak, front.
Fig. g: Turkish towelling bathing cloak, back.

LAWN TENNIS APRONS; CREWEL WORK *(8.6.1881, p. 500).* **Figs. a–c.**

LAWN TENNIS COSTUME WITH PO-LONAISE AND TRIMMED SKIRT *(8.20. 1881, p. 533).* **Fig. d.**

AESTHETIC DRESS (*11.19.1881, p. 749*). **Fig. a:** this costume is a reproduction of the Ancient Greek dress. It may be made of any soft flowing fabric, of silk or of wool, and is shown in yellow-greens, deep yellow, greenish-blue, and white. The dress illustrated is of white Surah and is all in one piece, being made of five long breadths sewed together and hemmed at the top and bottom. It is then suspended from the shoulders by cameo brooches that catch the top together, leaving sufficient space between for the head to pass through; the edges beyond this then droop down behind the arms as sleeves. A

a

girdle of ribbon is first passed over the shoulders crossed in the back, and straight under the arms in front; it is then easily tied around the waist, and the robe is pulled through the girdle far enough to let the upper part droop over it, and to bring the lower edge even with the floor. Vines of sunflowers, lilies or daisies are wrought up the back and front in South Kensington embroidery, or else they are painted by hand. **Fig. b:** this graceful Neo-Greek costume combines the classic characteristics with the requirements of modern fashion. It is composed of pale blue cashmere draped over a train of white cashmere, and

b

trimmed with gold embroidery done in a Greek key pattern. The blue bodice has transparent sleeves of white pineapple silk, opened in diamond spaces on the outer arm, and edged with gilt braid. The pointed Greek apron is sewed permanently to the waist, and the back has softly draped square breadths falling low on the square train of white cashmere. Pleatings of white satin are at the foot; white pineapple silk is gathered inside the square neck. Etruscan gold necklace and bracelets, being a reproduction of the gold ornaments excavated by Professor Schliemann. Gold braid forms Greek fillets on hair.

c

White satin shoes. **Fig. c:** this Early English dress is made of brick red satin, and has full frills of white muslin at the throat and wrists. The short round waist has a wide belt with a sash bow at the back. The tight sleeves have a large full puff at the top that is high on the shoulders. The full skirt of six straight breadths of satin has an old-fashioned shirred ruche across the three front breadths, while the back breadths are without trimming. Box-pleated frill of satin around the neck.

a   *b*   *c*   *d*   *e*   *f*   *g*   *h*   *i*   *j*

k   l   m   n   o

WINTER   COSTUMES   *(10.29.1881,*
pp. 696–697).
Fig. a: satin de Lyon cloak.
Fig. b: cashmere and moiré dress.
Fig. c: brocaded satin cloak.
Fig. d: dress for girl from 4 to 6 years old.
Fig. e: coat for girl from 5 to 10 years old.
Fig. f: plush jacket.
Fig. g: walking coat for girl from 4 to 6 years
old.
Fig. h: dress for girl from 4 to 9 years old.
Fig. i: cashmere and moiré dress.
Fig. j: suit for boy from 4 to 9 years.
Fig. k: brocaded velvet cloak.
Fig. l: English homespun mantle.
Fig. m: dress for girl from 9 to 11 years old.
Fig. n: satin serge cloak.
Fig. o: plush cloak.

LACE AND JET PELERINE *(9.24.1881, p. 613).* This pelerine consists of a gauze foundation, which is covered row upon row with gathered black Spanish lace. The neck is edged with a jet border and with jet leaves, which encircle a full lace ruche. Proceeding from the border at the neck, and falling over the rows of lace, are long and short jet sprays, that terminate in fringe at the lower edge. Manila Longchamps hat trimmed with a long ostrich plume and a cluster of roses.

a   b

EVENING AND STREET DRESSES
(11.26.1881, p. 754). **Fig. a:** this evening dress
has the new short skirt or quarter train. It
is of shaded turquoise blue lampas, trimmed
with turquoise satin and pale straw-colored
Surah. The two pleatings on the skirt are of
plain turquoise blue satin, the fans are straw-
colored Surah, and the principal part of the
dress is of lampas. The Surah in the fans is
doubled. Neyron red roses hold the upright
pleats of the lower part of the tablier. The
princesse corsage has pleated paniers in front
and on the sides, which extend to the back,
where the drapery falls in full breadths to the
foot of the skirt. The high corsage, which is

slightly pointed at the throat, and fastened
there by a single button, has an open space
in fan shape filled with Surah pleating, and
ornamented with a rose. The short sleeves
cross on top, and are bouffant. Long straw-
colored gloves. Pink wreath of roses around
the chignon, and a cluster low behind the ear.
Blue shoes, with buckles set with turquoises.
Fig. b: this walking suit is of dark green gros
grain, with cloth to match, and fuchsia red
cloth for facings and buttons. The skirt has
two tabliers, one of which is covered by three
deep pleatings, and the upper has upright folds
with a single narrow pleating. Two cloth
panels on each side are bordered with red

wool, and have large buttons covered with
the same. Two deep pleatings cross the back
of the skirt. The back drapery is very ample,
and there are full paniers on the sides. These
paniers cover the edge of the plain basque. The
sleeves have cuffs opened on the outside,
and bordered with red. The pelerine is of
green cloth lined with red, which is seen as
a border, and there are straight tabs to tie
it in front. Mull and lace trim the neck and
sleeves. Green gros grain bonnet, with green
plumes and red velvet roses. Long tan-colored
gloves.

VISITING AND RECEPTION TOILETTE *(1.28.1882, cover).* This graceful dress of Oriental sapphire blue lampas, with velvet to match, and a border of sea-otter. The lampas front is flat, with large hollow pleats on each side—not pressed flat—and which terminate in points at the foot. The fur border is set on straight beneath these pleats, and shows the points effectively. The velvet coat-bodice has seven deep points piped with satin. The neck is high, with a collar of satin set upon a fur collar that is pointed low on the bust. A very bouffant pouf of velvet is set under the middle point of the back, and terminates in two large points that fall low on the skirt. The sleeves are cut in points that rest on a fur border. Soft and fully gathered frill of guipure lace in the neck, down the front, and around the sleeves. Round hat of blue plush-felt, trimmed with shaded blue ostrich plumes. The blue velvet muff has a fur band around it. Tan-colored undressed kid gloves. Large satin pelisse, with fur border.

BUSTLES *(2.4.1881, p. 68).*
Fig. a: dimity bustle, front.
Fig. b: dimity bustle, back.
Fig. c: hair-cloth bustle.
Fig. d: dimity bustle.

CORSETS AND CAPS *(2.18.1882, p. 101).*
Fig. e: black satteen corset.
Fig. f: gray coutil corset.
Fig. g: lace and ribbon cap.
Fig. h: lace and ribbon cap.

BLACK MOTHER HUBBARD COLLAR
(2.18.1882, p. 101). **Fig. i.**

CORSETS *(10.21.1882, p. 661).*
Fig. j: spoon-bill corset.
Fig. k: lady's corset, front.
Fig. l: lady's corset, back.

FOULARD PETTICOAT *(10.21.1882, p. 661).*
Fig. m.

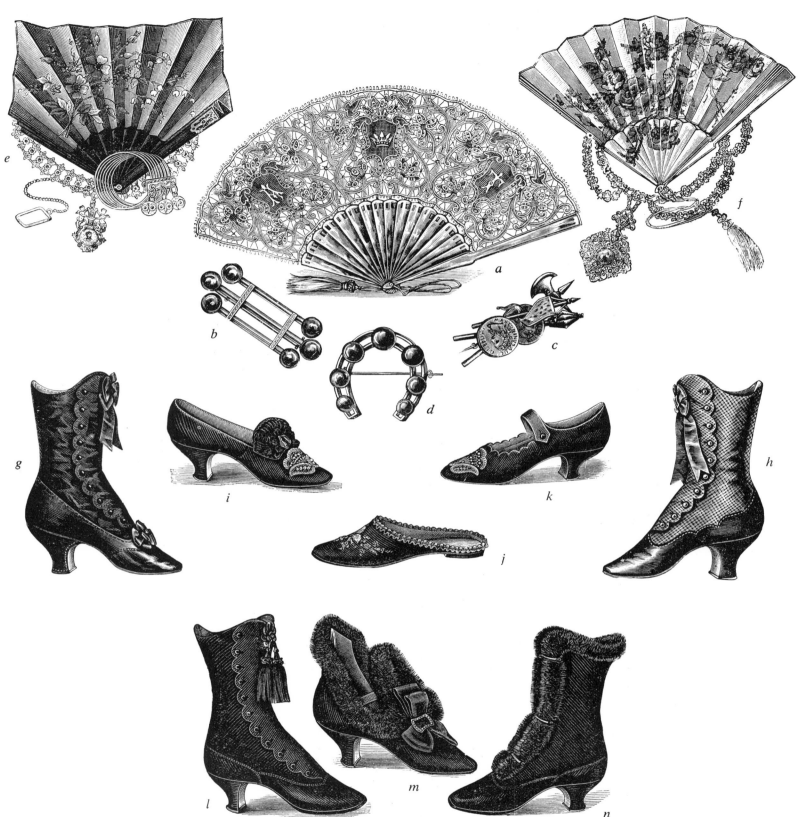

POINT LACE FAN (2.11.1882, p. 85). **Fig. a.**

FANS AND JEWELRY (11.18.1882, pp. 728–729). **Fig. e:** the square fan has an ebonized frame with silver ornamentation. The leaf is of pale olive satin, with a spray of flowers in natural colors painted on it, and a plain black satin lining. The necklace is composed of links in combined gold and platina, with a lapis lazuli at the center. The pendant, of gold and lapis lazuli, bears a Roman silver coin. The bangle bracelet is of gold and silver hoops from which three owl heads hang. **Fig. f:** the fan has ivory sticks and a white gros grain leaf decorated with large roses and foliage in hand-painting. The silver necklace has a large pendant at the center of which a sapphire is set.

BROOCHES (2.11.1881, p. 85).
Fig. b: a pendulum, or bar and ball pin.
Fig. c: representing a group of ancient coins and emblems.
Fig. d: a variation of the familiar horseshoe.

LADY'S WALKING BOOTS (7.15.1882, p. 437). **Figs. g and h.**

BOOTS, SHOES AND SLIPPERS (1.21.1882, p. 36).
Fig. i: satin slipper.
Fig. j: Turkish slipper.
Fig. k: embroidered kid slipper.
Fig. l: cloth walking boot.
Fig. m: kid carriage shoe.
Fig. n: cloth walking boot.

CLOAKS (*1.21.1882, p. 36*).
Fig. a: camel's-hair opera cloak.
Fig. b: brocade opera cloak.

BALL TOILETTE *(2.11.1882, cover).* This elegant dress is of magnolia satin with rosy tints, embroidered with beads of many colors. The long satin train is trimmed on the edge with two satin pleatings, with a double shirred ruche above them. The top of the train is gathered twice to form two bouffant puffs below the waist. The sides of the skirt are ornamented by a deep flounce of the satin, shirred at the top, and forming a panel as it hangs closely to the skirt. The tablier is a rich embroidery of beads and silk, terminated at the foot by two pleatings of the satin, which stop at the sides where the wide flounce begins. The long pointed corsage is very short on the hips and is laced behind. It is a low square in front and round behind, ornamented on the point, up the front, and on the back with embroidery like that of the tablier. The embroidered epaulets rest on satin and lisse pleatings that form the sleeves. A jardinière of variegated roses is on one shoulder, A bow of satin ribbon is on the corsage front. Louis XV fan. Roses in the coiffure. Magnolia satin shoes, with buckles of rubies and diamonds. Parure of damonds and rubies.

a   *b*

SPRING COSTUMES *(3.11.1882, cover).* **Fig. a:** pointed bodice and trimmed skirt. This new and graceful costume is made of cashmere of the new partridge plume color, trimmed with Havana brown embroidery. The foundation skirt of silk is covered in front by a draped apron, terminated by an embroidered band, not cut off, but descending to the foot, where it is ornamented by a shell ruche. A second drapery is at the top of the skirt; this is embroidered in the same manner on the left side, and on the right side a band

is set on. In the back is a draped breadth, embroidered on one side with a band mixed in the pouf. The corsage is pointed behind and before, and short on the hips; it is fastened with a "fly" and trimmed with two rows of buttons. Brocaded band on the left and on the right side, beginning with the seam under the arm. Revers collar of embroidery. Close sleeve, with embroidered cuff. Embroidered satin bonnet, trimmed with plumes and strings of satin ribbon. Feather muff, with a bird-of-paradise upon it. **Fig. b:** carmago waist and

panier skirt. This suit is made of cream-colored satine, with figured flounces and border. The Carmago waist is pointed in front and round behind, with open V neck, and close sleeves with a puff at the top. The skirt has three deep flounces in front, and two of these extend all around it. Narrow pleating of brown satine separates these flounces. The paniers meet a full puffed drapery that covers the back breadths. Tuscan straw bonnet, with yellow daisies, buff ribbon, and an ostrich plume for trimming.

a   *b*

SPRING COSTUMES *(4.29.1882, cover).* **Fig. a:** pointed basque, revers panier, and pleated skirt. This stylish costume is of plain dark green wool, combined with moiré striped wool showing lighter green shades. The basque is of simple shape, bordered with the stripe, and with puffs on the collar and cuffs. The revers paniers of the stripes are attached to the belt, then shirred lower down, then turned upward from the lowest edge, and caught together with loops in the middle of the back. The front has two deep double box-pleatings, one of which goes around the skirt, trimmed with moiré borders. Below this is a pouf of the plain wool, and a box-pleating at the foot made of the moiré stripe. Manila poke with lace edge, trimmed with dark green faille, shaded green feathers, and a single dark red rose. **Fib. b:** pelerine basque, double paniers, and trimmed skirt. Several new features are shown in this costume, viz., the pointed basque short on the hips, the new pelerine, and the very bouffant double paniers that show the outlines of French dresses now furnished with a pillow bustle. The material is plain bronze satin combined with wide moiré-striped bronze satin, and trimmed with velvet of the same shade. The plain satin skirt is held in double pleats that are shirred at the knees as well as at the top. There are two kinds of paniers, one of curtain shape shirred below the belt, and the other forming very bouffant back drapery. The striped basque is pointed back and front, and very short on the hips, being turned up on the sides, and trimmed with a velvet fold. A little pelerine fichu shaped in ''swallow-tail'' style behind trims the shoulders, and is finished with bias velvet folded quite narrow on the top, a bow on the bosom, and a lace frill with jabot in front. Half-long sleeves, with velvet fold curved up the outer seam. Rose-colored moiré poke bonnet, shirred inside, and trimmed with white and rose plumes. Long tan-colored Saxe gloves.

WATTEAU WRAPPER, BACK AND FRONT *(5.27.1882, cover).* The wrapper, which is in close-fitting princesse shape, is made of pale blue cashmere. The back is furnished with a broad Watteau fold, which expands into a long full train. The front of the skirt is covered from waist to hem with gradually widening cream lace ruffles, simulating a petticoat. Lace jabots, which extend from the throat to the hem, slanting outward from the waist, cover the ends of the ruffles. Long-looped satin ribbon bows are at the throat and waist and on the elbow sleeves.

OUTDOOR COSTUMES FOR WO-
MEN AND CHILDREN (*5.6.1882, pp.
280–281*).
Fig. a: French bunting dress with batiste
  embroidery.
Fig. b: Sicilienne visite.
Fig. c: embroidered camel's-hair dress.
Fig. d: cheviot jacket.
Fig. e: dress for girl from 4 to 6 years old.
Fig. f: grenadine dress and satin merveilleux
  mantle.
Fig. g: dress for girl from 3 to 5 years old.
Fig. h: walking coat for girl from 4 to 6 years
  old.
Fig. i: virginie cloth dress.
Fig. j: satin duchesse mantle.
Fig. k: velvet gauze mantle.
Fig. l: dress for girl from 7 to 9 years old.
Fig. m: satin soleil and moiré mantle.

j   *k*   *l*   *m*

a   *b*

COACHING AND COUNTRY TOILETTES (7.22.1882, p. 453). **Fig. a:** this gay coaching toilette has a skirt and basque of cream-colored *poult de soie* strewn with poppies and foliage, and an over-skirt of cream-tinted Flanders lace. The skirt has two lace pleatings headed by a shell ruche of lace. The over-skirt, made of breadths of the lace is draped in very full pleats, edged with a frill of lace, is caught up by a large faille bow on each side, and falls in "floods of drapery" behind. The corsage, pointed in back and front, has two bias folds near its edge, and a full frill of lace. The sleeves have a lace puff at the top, and ruffles below. A very small cape of lace completes this dress. Hat of twine straw, lined with black velvet and lace; roses under the brim, and pink ostrich tips outside. Parasol of beige-colored silk, trimmed with Flanders lace. Long chamois gloves. **Fig. b:** this elegant and simple country toilette is made of *étamine*, a new linen canvas of ficelle-color, with embroidery done on the fabric over ficelle-color faille and golden brown satin. The brown satin skirt has two rows of round pleats that are not adjusted; wide ficelle embroidery is the trimming. The long basque of the étamine is made over ficelle faille, and has a vest and sash of the brown satin. The sash is hidden under the basque on one side, and crosses it on the other, falling thence amid the fullness of the back of the basque. Three folds cross the top of the vest. Deep Byron collar and square cuffs of embroidery, with pompons on the cuffs. Parasol of the étamine, trimmed with ficelle lace, and lined with satin. Duchesse de Berri bonnet of Manila, faced with brown velvet, and trimmed with lilacs, Brown velvet strings.

a *b*

AUTUMN AND WINTER TOILETTES *(10.28.1882, cover).* **Fig. a:** this elegant visiting toilette is composed of a black and red lampas basque, and skirt of black satin trimmed with Chantilly lace. The soft black satin of the skirt has three flounces, each trimmed with lace, and draped unequally and very artistically. The habit basque of lampas is trimmed on the chest with a large shell ruche of Chantilly lace, which also forms the collar; the sides of the basque are short, the front is slightly pointed, and the back has very long tabs of great pleats, doubled to give them greater amplitude. A jabot of lace trims the sides and back, and there are bows of satin

ribbon set on the sides of the tournure and sleeves, trimmed with lace and ribbons. Black lace bonnet, with bright red velvet lining, and cluster of chrysanthemums. **Fig. b:** a gay Parisian costume, with a skirt and guimpe of India cashmere like that used for shawls, with an over-dress of Amazon cloth of the new gray-blue shade called *nuit de France.* The round skirt in large pleats shows stripes of the plain cashmere of bright Turkey red, and a border of the same at the foot, while the main parts are figured; below this is a pleating of plain blue cloth. Bows of blue velvet ribbon trim the front. The cloth body is pointed back and front and has the drapery sewed to its

edge, and festooned to form short side paniers, with long slender fullness behind. The guimpe of gay cashmere is very wide and full, and is continued in a panier scarf that is seen only on one side of the front; three bars of blue velvet ribbon are pointed in V shape across the guimpe. Close cloth sleeves with small puffs of velvet and of cashmere. The blue velvet bonnet has velvet pleating on the brim, velvet strings tied in a large bow, a velvet band with buckle, and a bunch of marigolds. Light tan-colored undressed kid gloves. Red parasol fastened with a blue velvet ribbon and a bow.

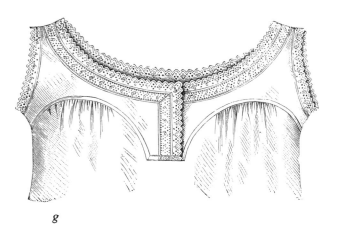

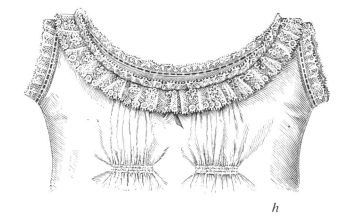

i *j* *k*

LINGERIE *(10.2.1882, pp. 548–549).*
Fig. a: lady's muslin petticoat.
Fig. b: lady's muslin petticoat.
Fig. c: lace chemise yoke and sleeves.
Fig. d: lady's silk stocking.
Fig. e: lady's silk stocking.

Fig. f: lady's combing sacque.
Fig. g: lady's chemise.
Fig. h: lady's chemise.
Fig. i: white cambric wrapper.
Fig. j: linen lawn morning gown, back.
Fig. k: linen lawn morning gown, front.

III

RETURN OF THE BUSTLE

1883-1890

One of the prime forces of change is ennui. In fashion it often manifests itself as a dissatisfaction with the original shape of the body and seeks expression in a wide variety of anatomical constrictions and distensions. Corsets have changed the shape of the torso by deforming the rib cage and displacing flesh. Devices such as farthingales, hoops and bustles have artificially expanded lower portions of the body so that a whole new form was created, bearing little resemblance to the hips and legs concealed by them.

Of these deviations from the natural, none is so difficult for the modern eye to justify in terms of esthetics, comfort or practicality as the form considered fashionable in the mid-1880s (Autumn Toilettes, p. 159; Street and In-door Toilettes, p. 162; Spring Suits, p. 175; Ladies' Dresses, p. 178; Visiting Toilettes, p. 190). The knees had been freed by this time, and the trains for day disappeared for easier walking, but the weight of these costumes and the structures needed to support the huge rear extension added little to increase mobility. Many of the fabrics were upholstery-like in quality, made even heavier by the profuse use of beading, fringes, braids and furs (Dinner and Evening Toilettes, pp. 164–165; Spring Wrappings, p. 181; Visiting Toilettes, p. 199). Some dresses alone weighed over ten pounds. Summer costumes were made of lighter material, but they were no less layered.

Yet it was during this period that women pushed further into the area of sports, invading some that had been wholly the domain of men, such as yachting and fencing (Fig. b, Gowns, p. 176; Ladies' Class, p. 211). For sportswear few concessions were made in design. Details and trimmings were simplified or eliminated, but to remain fashionable on the tennis court or on a yacht, a lady still had to wear her corset and bustle, no matter how strenuous her activity (Yachting and Tennis Gowns, pp. 196–197). Only bathing costumes escaped them (Beach and Bathing Dresses, p. 179).

Compared with the bustle of the early 1870s, which had soft curves, the silhouette of the mid-1880s seems to have a hard edge. When viewed in profile, it appears to be a small triangle set forward on a very large square (Fig. b, Winter Wrappings, p. 174; Dinner and Reception Toilettes, p. 192). As the skirt increased in volume, for day use the bodice became plainer, and was even tailored on occasions (Spring Styles, p. 153; Autumn Costumes pp. 160–161; Autumn Walking Toilettes, pp. 172–173). For evening, the tops—sleeveless and low in back and front—became little more than corselets (Evening Gowns, pp. 154–155; Dinner Toilettes, pp. 164–165; 188–189). Hairstyles and hats and bonnets were peaked as though to complete the apex of the triangle (Hair-dressing, p. 180; Hats and Bonnets, p. 186; Accessories, p. 193; Winter Bonnets, p. 208). Headgear during this period was as ornate as the costumes. Along with flowers, ribbons and feathers, there was a strange taste for real birds as trimmings.

Growing out of the esthetic preferences of an era, stylistic elements found in costume also appear in decorative arts, particularly in interior furnishings. For example, in Dinner Dresses, pp. 150–151, the design of the curving wooden frame of the rocking chair, the pattern of the upholstery and the application of fringes are closely analogous in spirit to that of the costumes and accessories on the same page. In Dresses, Table and Jewel Case, pp. 182–183, the type of lace and system of draping on the dressing table are reflected on the gowns in the room. In Ladies' Walking and Evening Dresses, p. 163, the curves of the table legs parallel the shape of the skirts of the gowns next to it.

By 1889 the rear extension began to recede (Spring Toilettes, pp. 212–213; Spring Wrappings, pp. 214–215). Once again there was some talk of totally abolishing the bustle and adopting the loose classical Empire style of the early nineteenth century. The bustle, however, remained to fade on its own, giving way to a new interest in another part of the anatomy—the shoulders (Outdoor Toilettes, p. 216; The Surprise Dress, p. 217). "Sleeves have grown in size and importance of late, until now they are a prominent feature of dress" (May 4, 1889).

e

f

g

h

i

j

k

a

b

EVENING DRESSES, DINNER DRESSES, BALL DRESSES, ORNAMENTS AND CHAIR *(2.3.1883, pp. 72–73)*.

Fig. a: brocade and satin dress without adjustable train (see figs. i, f and m).

Fig. b: young lady's satin evening dress.

Fig. c: tulle and satin ball dress.

Fig. d: nun's veiling evening dress.

Fig. e: lace hood.

Fig. f: skirt of dress without train (see fig. i).

Fig. g: velvet and lace dinner dress.

Fig. h: Ottoman silk and velvet evening dress.

Fig. i: brocade and satin dress with adjustable train (see figs. a, f and m).

Fig. j: cloth dress with soutache embroidery.

Fig. k: cloth and velvet dress with fur trimming.

Fig. l: dress sleeves.

Fig. m: adjustable train for dress (see fig. i).

Fig. n: embroidered rocking chair.

Fig. o: fans, muff, hair and corsage bouquets and jewelry.

a   *b*   *c*   *d*

EVENING AND DINNER DRESSES *(2.3. 1883, pp. 72–73).*
Fig. a: satin and lace evening dress.
Fig. b: Ottoman silk and velvet evening dress.
Fig. c: velvet and lace dinner dress.
Fig. d: plain and damassé gauze evening dress.

a   *b*   *c*

SPRING STYLES *(2.10.1883, p. 92).* The illustrations on this page represent the earliest spring styles, both in designs and materials, and will be useful to the ladies who make up their light woolen dresses in advance of the spring, and devote their Lenten leisure to making and remodelling their summer dresses for the country. **Fig. a:** this graceful dress is of olive green foulard silk, with dark myrtle green shamrock leaves, and is trimmed with écru Oriental lace. This model is also excellent for very dressy cotton satteens that do not need to be washed often. **Fig. b:** this simple dress for early spring and summer is made of plain and checked Cheviot in terracotta, olive, strawberry red shades, seal brown, or black and white. **Fig. c:** this gay dress of cotton satteen has an écru ground strewn with clusters of pink carnations. The Marie Antoinette over-skirt is very bouffant, and is caught back in points on the sides. Two rows of the open Irish point embroidery are the trimmings. English straw bonnet, with pink roses and an écru ostrich plume.

EVENING AND BALL GOWNS *(2.17. 1883, pp. 104–105).*
Fig. a: tulle and satin ball dress.
Fig. b: satin and brocade evening dress.
Fig. c: gauze and lace ball dress.
Fig. d: dress for girl from 7 to 9 years old.
Fig. e: dress for girl from 8 to 10 years old.
Fig. f: dress for girl from 5 to 7 years old.
Fig. g: gauze and satin ball dress.
Fig. h: tarlatan and satin ball dress.
Fig. i: dress for girl from 3 to 4 years old.
Fig. j: tulle and satin evening dress.
Fig. k: brocade and satin merveilleux evening dress.

i   *j*   *k*

a   b   c   d   e   f   g

h   i   j

COSTUMES FOR WOMEN AND CHILDREN (*5.5.1883, pp. 280–281*).
Fig. a: Sicilienne visite.
Fig. b: cloth and velvet cloak.
Fig. c: dress of cashmere and Persian cloth, with cape.
Fig. d: cloak for girl from 3 to 7 years old.
Fig. e: dress for girl from 4 to 8 years old.
Fig. f: cashmere dress with shirred cape.
Fig. g: brocaded grenadine mantle.
Fig. h: cloth and moiré dress.
Fig. i: Ottoman silk mantle.
Fig. j: dress for girl from 3 to 7 years old.

a   *b*

SEA-SIDE AND WATERING-PLACE COSTUMES *(8.25.1883, cover).* **Fig. a:** seaside costume. This quaintly pretty dress is of cobalt blue wool, trimmed with red cotton embroidery on brown étamine or canvas. The short round skirt without flounces has large pleats fastened only at the belt, falling thence carelessly—not in set folds—trimmed with two borders of the embroidery. The new feature of this costume is the polonaise or blouse, called the carter's frock, which has the waist and skirt in one. This garment is shirred around the neck, and trimmed with a small collar of embroidery, and two curved bands on the front that form a horseshoe. This loose blouse is confined at the waist by a belt of red Russia leather, and is fastened under one side of the horseshoe below the collar in a

way that makes it difficult to tell how it is put on and where it is fastened. Hat of Sienna red glacé straw, trimmed with a small parrot and red ostrich plumes. Suède gloves of reddish tan-color. Parasol of Turkey red cotton with an étamine border and a bow of red ribbon on the handle. Low shoes and Russia leather red Balbriggans. **Fig. b:** watering-place costume. This beautiful dress is of violet summer velvet of the India amethyst shade, with an over-dress of écru embroidery on batiste. The velvet skirt is attached to the belt in large pleats that fall below in natural folds without being fastened. The over-skirt is of écru embroidery, trimmed with a deep flounce to match, and is draped high on the hips. The corsage is an open-worked écru jacket, adjusted closely behind and under the arms,

but flowing open in front over a chemise Russe of velvet that is pleated and puffed below the waist. A piece of velvet pleated, and with square corners, terminates the back. The corsage and chemise Russe are held together by a strap on the sides between the vest and the chemise Russe. Half-long sleeves of embroidery, trimmed with a pouf of velvet. Square cornered collar with a cravat bow. Hat of écru straw, trimmed with bands and bows of velvet and a cluster of corn-poppies. Long suede gloves. Écru China crape umbrella with flowers painted on it as a border, lined with green silk, and a knot of velvet ribbon on the bamboo club handle. Patent-leather shoes adorned with bows of black and strass buckles. Écru silk stockings with colored silks.

a   *b*

AUTUMN TOILETTES *(9.8.1883, cover).* **Fig. a:** the Dagmar costume. This handsome costume is of Russian green cashmere, with appliqué velvet leaves on the corsage, the apron, and the drapery bow. The cashmere basque is of simple shape, with pointed front, and smoothly fitted round back with the large bow of drapery set upon it. The bouffant sleeves are finished with a cuff of écru embroidery on guipure net. The round skirt is plain in front, and falls in loose kilt pleats behind. The apron of the figured stuff is attached to the belt of the lower skirt, and falls in lengthwise folds of plain goods to match those of the costume. Small bonnet of Russian green velvet, with a coronet front, back of which is a puff of yellow velvet, some velvet ribbon loops, and a yellow aigrette. Strings of velvet ribbon. Tan-colored Suède gloves. **Fig. b:** the Molière coat. This long coat is made of rough-finished Pékin wool with Czar brown stripes alternating with Venetian stripes in gay colors. Its peculiar feature is the full Molière vest of dull ottoman silk which is put on outside the buttons and shirred at top and bottom. It is worn to open over a pleated skirt of the material used for the vest. Black velvet hat, with fur-lined brim and cluster of ostrich tips. Gray Suède gloves. We are indebted to the courtesy of Messrs. Lord & Taylor for these models.

a   *b*

c

AUTUMN COSTUMES *(9.22.1883, p. 604).*
Fig. a: plain and brocaded wool costume. This
wool costume is a stylish arrangement of the
new camel's-hair brocaded figures of a darker
shade of brown than that of the plain ground.
The figured goods forms the plain basque,
with high-cut sleeves and pleated postilion;
the vest of the plain camel's-hair covers the
front edges of the lining, and is buttoned by
velvet buttons. Écru felt hat with very dark
red velvet trimming, and écru and salmon
ostrich tips. Embroidered collar and cuffs.
Tan-colored Suède gloves. **Fig. b:** ottoman
and velvet costume. This costume is composed of three different fabrics, viz., plain
ottoman silk for the basque, plain velvet for
the skirt, and ottoman silk with appliqué
velvet figures for the long over-skirt. The
color is dark gray-blue. The pointed basque
of ottoman silk has a Byron collar and cuffs
of blue velvet, and small flat velvet buttons.
Blue felt hat with dark red ostrich plumes.
Long tan-colored gloves. **Fig. c:** English tailor
suit. This tailor suit is of checked brown cloth
with a velvet collar and cuffs. The basque
is suitable for house or street; it is single-
breasted, with curved fronts and pleated back.
The neck is arranged to have a flat scarf inside
with a standing linen collar. A single breast
pocket for watch or eye-glasses is made
inside, with only a slit visible outside. The
apron of the over-skirt has one side turned
forward in a fish-wife revers, and the back
is very bouffantly draped. Soft felt hat of dark
golden brown, with wings of the English blue
jay stuck in the band. Brown castor gloves.

a   *b*

STREET AND IN-DOOR TOILETTES *(10.20.1883, cover).* **Fig. a:** velvet and cloth pelisse. This elegant Parisian wrap is a sleeveless pelisse of soft, fine, beige-colored cloth, with the upper part of gloxinia or golden brown velvet made to represent a shawl-shaped mantle. Ornaments and tassels of brown silk and chenille are on the sides and front of the pelisse, which has no other trimming. Dress of green silk. Brown velvet bonnet trimmed with loops and strings of scarlet ribbon. Brown and red ostrich tips curl forward from the crown, and a tea-rose is inside the brim. Long tan-colored Suède gloves. Brown umbrella with Japanese handle. Brown kid shoes and brown silk stockings. **Fig. b:** in-door toilette. This graceful dress for the house is of Sicilienne of the pale salmon shade called *aurore du Bengale,* with India embroidery on the fabric for the tablier, and trimmings of white lace and rosettes of ruby velvet ribbon. The front breadths and all the visible parts of the round skirt are embroidered in large palms of pale green and faded red shades. The high-shouldered sleeves reach to the elbow, where they have sabot frills of lace and a rosette of velvet. There is a narrow vest of the embroidery wrought in smaller palms, and a fichu of the lace that forms a small hood in the back, and drapes in the front. A high standing collar attached to the dress is also embroidered in a small design. *Petit abbé* shoes of navy blue kid, with gold buckles, and scarlet silk stockings. High coiffure, with an amber comb. Bengal rose at the throat.

a

b

LADIES' WALKING AND EVENING DRESSES *(12.1.1883, cover)*. **Fig. a:** this stylish French walking costume is made of golden brown wool combined with striped silk of this golden brown shade alternating with stripes of the new blue-gray called *grande clématite*. The round skirt has a brown wool pleating all around the foot; in front there is merely a pleating of the striped goods, but in the back this striped silk extends the whole length, and is caught very low down, and falls in pleatings below. The tunic-tablier of the brown wool is draped loosely and low on the skirt by *rosaces* of brown satin ribbon; there are two closely pleated flounces below this tablier.

The guimpe of striped silk is a bias piece gathered at the top, pleated broadly across the bust, and folded into a point at the waist line, where it is held by ribbon loops. The picturesque bonnet is of brown velvet, with irregularly indented front, lined with gray-blue silk; it is trimmed with loops of these materials and ostrich tips of the two colors of the dress. Suède gloves of light tan-color. Brown stockings, and patent-leather shoes. **Fig. b:** this charming evening toilette for a young lady has a short round skirt covered with pointed flounces of rose-colored faille and a waist and drapery of changeable rose and green faille, trimmed with green velvet

ribbon, puffed white silk muslin, and a cluster of flowers of many colors. The changeable silk drapery is pleated in scarfs on the side and held in place by large bows and loops of velvet ribbon. There is a green velvet ribbon down each side of the chemisette, and a dog-collar around the neck without lace above. The short puffed sleeve may be of muslin or of rows of lace, with a bracelet at the edge of the velvet ribbon, fastened by a buckle of diamonds like that on the dog-collar. Long gloves of the new fresh-butter shade. Gold bracelets. Fan of white crape spangled with gold. Rose-pink slippers, and pink silk stockings.

a

b

DINNER AND EVENING TOILETTES
(2.23.1884, p. 125). **Fig. a:** this elaborate
toilette for dinners, receptions, weddings, or
any full-dress occasion where a high-necked
dress may be worn, is composed of Sèvres
blue ciselé velvet, with a vest and skirt front
of straw-colored satin richly embroidered and
trimmed with Chantilly lace. The front of the
velvet basque opens over a narrow vest of
straw-colored satin, which is almost concealed by black lace. The small collar and
the ends of the long sleeves are of satin, with
lace ruffles. The epaulets are double frills of
lace held by richly beaded passementerie,
which falls in tassels behind and before. The
front breadth of the satin hangs in a drooping
puff, and the side-pleatings at the foot are
of plain satin—that is, without embroidery.
The Chantilly lace forms butterfly bows and
gathered frills that droop on the tablier. The
panels and the long square train are of the
ciselé velvet. **Fig. b:** this graceful evening
dress with a small train is made of sea-foam
green silk, trimmed with white lace and large
clusters of roses of variegated colors—pink,
cream, and deep red—held by *flots* of green
velvet or satin ribbon. A deep flounce of lace
crosses the front and falls upon a narrower
flounce. The low pointed corsage is of silk,
covered with lace put on smoothly as a transparent. A drapery of silk begins on the right
shoulder, crosses the front, and is lost under
the flowers of the left side. A smaller bouquet
is placed on the left of the corsage. The high
coiffure has a cluster of pink and green ostrich
tips. Painted silk fan. Silk stockings and satin
slippers the color of the dress.

a   *b*

c

d

SPRING COSTUMES *(3.22.1884, p. 188)*. The illustrations represent marked features of imported costumes of spring Cheviots, camel's-hair, and other woolen goods; among these is a new design for a tailor suit, a model of the accordion skirt, also of the quaint old style revived under the name of the "grandmother dress," and of a graceful Parisian toilette with the Molière coat-basque. **Fig. a:** tailor suit. **Fig. b:** pointed Plastron-basque, draped over-skirt, and accordion. **Fig. c:** grandmother dress. **Fig. d:** Molière coat-basque trimmed skirt.

a   b   c   f   d   e   g   h

OUTERWEAR *(4.26.1884, pp. 264–265).*
Fig. a: figured cloth pelisse.
Fig. b: Ottoman silk mantle.
Fig. c: diagonal cloth mantle.
Fig. d: pleated shoulder cape.
Fig. e: coat for girl from 3 to 5 years old.
Fig. f: kilt suit for boy from 2 to 3 years old.
Fig. g: Ottoman silk visite.
Fig. h: dress for girl from 4 to 6 years old.
Fig. i: long cloak of plain and figured cloth.
Fig. j: suit for boy from 3 to 5 years old.
Fig. k: young lady's cloth jacket.
Fig. l: dress for girl from 6 to 8 years old.

i   *j*   *k*   *l*

a   *b*

SUMMER TOILETTES *(8.2.1884, cover).*
Fig. a: sea-side toilette. This graceful costume for the sea-side has a skirt of soft white wool étamine, with an over-dress of striped silk, having dark red stripes on a white ground. The étamine skirt has large box pleats that are festooned near the lower edge by being caught up in a bunch of small pleats between two length-wise pleats; these droop upon a gathered flounce that is held in three tucks. The half-long sleeves have pleated revers of folds laid to show the stripes, with triple ends

across the wrists. The collar and frills on the sleeves are pleated batiste. Dark straw round hat, trimmed with velvet and flowers. Red silk umbrella, trimmed with cream-colored lace. **Fig. b:** watering-place toilette. This tasteful dress for the house is composed of white lace and pink Pompadour foulard, trimmed with rose-pink ribbons. The skirt is covered with lace flounces across the front and loosely pleated piece-lace on the sides. A large *flot* (or loops and ends of ribbon in a cluster) is placed on the front just below

the fully wrinkled tablier of foulard which is edged with a frill of lace. The foulard corsage has a short point in front, and is trimmed by a large bow of long loops on the side. Down the front are ribbon revers forming bretelles that edge a vest made of rows of the lace laid outside the foulard. Sleeves half-long, trimmed with a little jabot of lace and a small bow of ribbon set on inside the arm. A rosette of pink ribbon is in the hair. Pink shoes and stockings.

a   *b*

SUMMER TOILETTES *(8.23.1884, cover).*
Fig. a: this elegant visiting toilette is made
of heliotrope foulard with large figures of various colors draped over a skirt of plain heliotrope, trimmed with velvet and *bise* écru lace.
The round skirt has five gathered flounces of
lace, headed by wide bands or folds of heliotrope velvet; four of these are posed in points
to form a tablier. An independent breadth of
the foulard falls from the belt, and turns to
form drapery on the left side. The polonaise
is alike on both sides. The belt of velvet is
pointed; the high collar and pointed plastron
are also of velvet. The guimpe-vest is of écru
net or of étamine; it is slightly gathered at
top and bottom, and this transparent material
is laid over a foulard corsage of the heliotrope

shade. At the back the polonaise is pleated
as in front, and lies smoothly on the plain
back of the corsage beneath. Filigree or lace
straw bonnet, trimmed with a bouquet of
flowers of many colors. Heliotrope foulard
umbrella, with a border figured like the dress;
velvet bow on the handle. **Fig. b:** this tasteful
Parisian walking dress is made of a new cotton
fabric called *toile de Jouy;* the ground is India
red, and the figures are large branches of
lighter shades. The trimmings are pleated *bise*
lace, red velvet, and satin ribbon. The round
skirt is bordered with a pleating of wide écru
lace, and there is a double shell trimming of
lace up the front, with pleatings between, and
long loops of ribbon. The short round tunic
is edged with a deep pleating, on which are

three rows of pleated lace. The corsage is
a basque slightly rounded in front; the back
and the side forms are trimmed with lace; the
front side is detached at the end, and hangs
independent of the front. The neck opens in
V shape, and has a revers collar of dark red
velvet, and the sleeves have also velvet revers
for cuffs. A large jabot of lace and loops of
ribbon trims the front. Long sleeves stuffed
at the top. Filigree straw hat bordered with
a red velvet puff, and trimmed with pale pink
roses and cream-colored plumes. Suède
gloves of pearl gray shade. Red stockings and
black shoes. Red umbrella, trimmed with
pleated lace.

a　　　　　　　　　　　　　　　*b*　　　　　　　　　　　　　　　*c*

d

AUTUMN WALKING TOILETTES
(9.6.1884, p. 571). These illustrations represent the costumes imported for early autumn, and embody many novel features, such as the short jacket with braided vest, the princesse back, the round waist with revers and belt, draperies with short front and full back in bouffant style, whether straight or looped, and plain skirts without flounces. In the original these dresses are made of the new wool stuffs that are preferred for walking toilettes, but the designs are also appropriate for combinations of silk with velvet, or any of the rich fabrics used for carriage costumes. We are indebted to the courtesy of Messrs. Lord & Taylor for these tasteful models. **Fig. a:** round waist, plain skirt, and short drapery. **Fig. b:** short jacket with vest, apron over-skirt, and bordered skirt. **Fig. c:** pointed basque, and panel skirt with straight back. **Fig. d:** princesse dress.

a   *b*

WINTER WRAPPINGS (*11.15.1884, p. 722*). **Fig. a:** blouse casaque. This graceful cloak is of light gray cloth trimmed with passementerie and Angora wool lace of the same shade. The front of the waist is gathered to form a blouse or chemisette, and is crossed with bars of passementerie. The front of the skirt is pleated, the sides are flat, and behind are large pleats crossed with two rows of passementerie. Large pleated sleeves with pas-

sementerie wristband and two frills of gray wool lace. **Fig. b:** mantle redingote. This redingote is of soft gray velvet trimmed with natural beaver and wide gray galloon. It is fitted to the figure in the back, but hangs loose and straight in front. The middle seam of the back of the skirt has a large pleat on each side, and falls open to show a red satin lining. The beaver fur is down each side sloping to a point, falls straight down the fronts, forms

the collar, and borders the pagoda sleeves. The seams in the back of the waist have the velvet laid over and stitched to represent very fine pleats. The wide galloon is turned under to form points on the panel-shaped sides and up the front. The red velvet pleating at the foot is all that is seen of the dress beneath. Gray velvet hat, faced with red velvet and trimmed with red plumes and a windmill bow.

a

b

SPRING WALKING SUITS *(3.21.1885, cover).* **Fig. a:** this graceful dress has a pleating of plain blue camel's-hair, with an overskirt of figured wool carried plain around the lower skirt, and lapped in a curve on one side, where the end is drawn up to the belt. The waist of figured goods is pointed in front and behind, and opens over a guimpe of the plain wool, which laps to one side, and forms a short lambrequin drapery. Gilt buckles on the corsage. Écru straw hat, trimmed with blue velvet and écru plumes. Tan-colored Suède gloves and blue parasol. **Fig. b:** this stylish walking suit for spring is of campanule or bluebell gray wool, trimmed with steel and silver galloon. The round skirt is bordered with a frill of small separated pleats, headed by seven rows of the mixed steel and silver braid, which has the effect of being nearly white. The jacket is adjusted behind and is loose in front, and may have a fitted front lining to hold it in place, or else merely a wide belt set in the seams under the arms. Straw bonnet of the new blue-gray, trimmed with white wool lace and pink and gray feathers.

a   *b*   *c*

d

GOWNS FROM THE TROUSSEAU OF THE PRINCESS BEATRICE *(5.16.1885, p. 325).* These illustrations represent some of the cloth gowns that form part of the trousseau of the Princess Beatrice of England. They are of woolen stuffs of light weight, suitable for summer and autumn, and are furnished us by the makers, the Messrs. Redfern. **Fig. a:** this traveling gown is made of rough English cloth in navy blue and stripes of very narrow width. The basque has a notched collar like that in men's morning coats, and is worn with a cravat of dull red silk; the back rests smoothly on the tournure, and is very short. The Tam o'Shanter cap is of dark red cloth, with a blue quill thrust through it. Tan-colored gloves. High white linen collar and narrow cuffs. **Fig. b:** this gown for yachting and for tennis is of cream white flannelette, with turquoise blue wool inlaid in small pleats between the large box pleats of the skirt. Sailor hat of rough white straw, with blue canvas ribbon band. **Fig. c:** this tasteful gown is of dark red habit cloth, with ottoman silk of the same shade forming the vest, and inlaid between the wide box pleats of the skirt. The basque is sharply pointed in front and short on the hips, and pleated like a habit in the back. The silk vest laps over the fastening of the lining in one piece, in Breton fashion, and has revers at the upper part; the officer's collar also has silk in front. English turban of the red silk laid in folds, and ornamented with a gilt pin. **Fig. d:** this dress has a waist of navy blue webbing, with blue serge skirts, and trimming of crimson and blue blocks. A crimson vest is fastened by two rows of pale blue buttons.

a   b   c

LADIES' HOUSE AND STREET DRESSES (*11.1.1884, p. 700*). **Fig. a:** this graceful autumn suit for a young lady is composed of striped wool and golden brown shades, combined with plain brown wool and dark blue velvet. The striped wool is placed flat on the front and sides, with narrow écru pleating at the foot. Blue velvet is used for the fan-pleating down the middle of the front and to form the pleated back breadths. The short wrinkled apron over-skirt is of plain brown wool. The striped corsage has a small puff around it, and is trimmed with a blue velvet vest and high velvet collar. Puffed cuff on the sleeves. **Fig. b:** this reception dress is of very light beige-colored Sicilienne, trimmed with golden brown velvet. The round skirt has a border of large pleats of Sicilienne with wide spaces between; the tablier is of the same material, trimmed on the lower edge by shells of embroidery caught up by lengthwise bands of the golden brown velvet, which droop at the foot in a loop and notched end. Short loops are at the top. The back is of long straight breadths sewed to the basque like a redingote, and trimmed up each side with an embroidered revers that is widest at the top. A large velvet bow defines the back. Variegated roses for the corsage bouquet, and two roses in the hair. Long loose écru undressed kid gloves. Brown shoes to match the velvet. **Fig. c:** this walking costume has a gros grain skirt of blue-gray shade, laid in large flat pleats that open over a fan pleating which falls on a narrow box-pleated frill at the foot. The polonaise is of velvet with small colored figures upon it, and is festooned to form a tablier and a side lambrequin, with bouffant back drapery. There is a pleated silk vest in front, with sash bows of the same on one side. Felt hat with velvet bands around the crown and an aigrette in front. Brown fur muff and tan Suède gloves.

a   *b*   *c*   *d*   *e*

BEACH AND BATHING DRESSES *(7.4.*
1885, cover).
Fig. a: lady's morning dress.
Fig. b: young girl's dress.
Fig. c: lady's bathing suit and cap.
Fig. d: lady's bathing suit and cloak.
Fig. e: child's bathing dress.
Fig. f: lady's bathing suit and cloak.

ACCESSORIES *(8.25.1885, p. 168).*
Fig. a: sun-umbrella.
Fig. b: lace parasol.
Fig. c: embroidered parasol.
Fig. d: sun-umbrella.
Fig. e: bonnet bouquet.
Fig. f: bonnet bouquet.
Fig. g: leather belt.

HAIR-DRESSING *(9.12.1885, p. 596).*
Fig. h: bridal or evening coiffure.
Fig. i: coiffure, front.
Fig. j: coiffure, back.
Fig. k: coiffure.

a

b

c

SPRING WRAPPINGS *(4.25.1885, cover)*.
Fig. a: plain and figured velvet mantle.
Fig. b: repped silk jacket.
Fig. c: plain and figured velvet mantle.

e   *f*

DRESSES, TABLE AND JEWEL CASE
(9.12.1885, p. 597).
Fig. a: bordered veiling dress.
Fig. b: brocade and lace dress.
Fig. c: corsage with fichu drapery.
Fig. d: bengaline silk dress.
Fig. e: silk and lace dress.
Fig. f: toilette table.
Fig. g: stand with jewel case.

h   *i*   *j*   *k*

LADIES' WINTER WRAPPINGS *(10.31.*
1885, pp. 704–705).
Fig. a: repped silk cloak.
Fig. b: camel's-hair cloth cloak, back (see
    fig. i).
Fig. c: plain and figured velvet cloak (see
    fig. f).
Fig. d: plush jacket with flowing sleeves.
Fig. e: girl's dress.
Fig. f: plain and figured velvet cloak.
Fig. g: cloth jacket.
Fig. h: cloth and velvet cloak.
Fig. i: camel's-hair cloth coat, front (see
    fig. b).
Fig. j: frock for girl from 3 to 5 years old.
Fig. k: cloth and striped velvet cloak.

HATS AND BONNETS *(11.5.1885, p. 772).*
Fig. a: velvet round hat.
Fig. b: velvet bonnet.
Fig. c: embroidered bonnet.
Fig. d: velvet round hat.
Fig. e: bonnet for girl from 3 to 5 years old.

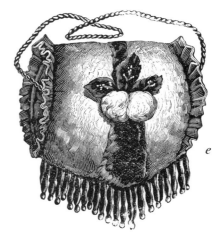

FUR AND FUR TRIMMING *(12.12.1885, p. 804).*
Fig. a: fur-trimmed cloth costume, back.
Fig. b: fur-trimmed cloth costume, front.
Fig. c: plush cloak with fur trimming.
Fig. d: young girl's seal turban.
Fig. e: young girl's seal muff.

g   *h*   *i*   *j*   *k*

DINNER AND EVENING TOILETTES
(1.29.1887, pp. 80–81).
Fig. a: young lady's tulle dress.
Fig. b: silk and tulle dress.
Fig. c: young girl's mull dress.
Fig. d: satin and lace dress.
Fig. e: velvet and lace dress.
Fig. f: crêpe de chine and velvet dress.
Fig. g: brocaded tulle dress.
Fig. h: embroidered surah dress.
Fig. i: gauze dress.
Fig. j: faille and lace dress.
Fig. k: satin dress.

a

b

VISITING TOILETTES *(2.5.1887, p. 93).*
Fig. a: this rich costume for paying visits has a dress of heliotrope faille française and a mantle of plush of a deeper shade, trimmed with the white musk-rat fur now in favor in Paris. The beauty of the long over-skirt is in its simple drapery being prettily caught up on the left side, while the back falls nearly plain, with short wing-like folds at the top. The visite of heliotrope plush has bead and chenille ornaments forming a V in front and back, with strands of the heliotrope-colored beads on the shoulders, and tufts of chenille on the fronts. The fur forms the high collar, borders the sleeves, and edges the back under the postillion-pleated basque. High plush round hat of dark heliotrope shade, with tuft of ostrich tips held by small bow of primrose satin. **Fig. b:** this graceful design represents some of the new features of French walking dresses. It is made of Suède-colored ladies'-cloth combined with plaid brown and Suède velvet. The velvet serves for the round skirt, and for the Louis Quatorze coat, which is made on and forms part of a polonaise of the Suède cloth. Plain brown velvet is used for the revers, cuffs, and collar, and also for trimming the round hat of Suède felt. The crown of the hat is covered with a panache composed of ostrich tips and wings shaded from Suède to dark brown.

a

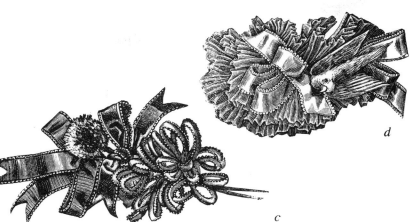

c

d

b

e

EVENING SLIPPERS, BOOT, CLOTH COLLAR AND CUFF *(2.5.1887, p. 117).* **Fig. a:** the bronze kid slipper on the left of the cut is beaded with bronze beads on the low vamp. The bronze kid boot on the right is widely open on the front and laced with silk lacing. The vamp is beaded, and trimmed with a beaded rosette. A black patent-leather slipper is shown in the background, which is beaded with gold, steel, and gray and white pearl beads. A bow of black watered ribbon is set on the beaded vamp, and another is on the elastic strap which holds the slipper on the instep. **Fig. b:** this standing collar and cuff, which are to be basted inside the neck and wrists of a tailor dress, consist of two pinked bands of cloth, the outer écru, the inner dark blue, which is stitched with lines of dark blue silk.

HAIR ORNAMENTS *(4.16.1887, p. 280).* **Fig. c:** this ornament consists of pleated frills of light blue ribbon, and a small yellow bird. **Fig. d:** this hair bow is composed of knots of red double-faced velvet and gros grain ribbon, a red chenille pompon, and tufts of loops of narrow red feather-edged ribbon.

PARASOLS *(4.16.1887, p. 280).* **Fig. e:** the large open parasol at the left of this group has a cover formed of two square silk handkerchiefs showing colored Japanese floral designs on light-tinted ground. A ruche of lace encircles the ferrul, and the carved handle is decorated with a cluster of pompons. Above this parasol is one with a cover of black Chantilly lace mounted on heliotrope silk. The stick has a hammered metal ball for the handle. Next is a striped parasol in alternate brown satin and brown and gold barred stripes, with a curved handle. To the right is shown a lace parasol with a pagoda-shaped frame à la Pompadour. It is made in both black and white lace. Bows of feather-edged ribbon trim the outside and the handle. Grouped with this is a parasol of écru and red striped silk, with a border of red stripes and a carved handle.

TORTOISE-SHELL COMB AND HAIR-PINS *(5.14.1887, p. 353).* **Figs. f and g.**

f

g

a   *b*

DINNER AND RECEPTION TOILETTES
(4.2.1887, p. 244). **Fig. a:** this dress for receptions at home is of light golden brown Bengaline over a lampas skirt that has a cream ground, on which are green, yellow, and dull red figures, and the garniture of wine-colored velvet. The sides of the dress are of lampas, and the flat front has a vest and tablier in continuous pieces fastened by an invisible piece underneath. The fronts of the corsage are of the Bengaline, lengthened as a demi-polonaise, in low points on the skirt, held by a bow of wine-colored velvet. In the back the Bengaline skirt is draped under the pointed basque of Bengaline, and falls in poufs lower down. Suède gloves. Silk stockings in the color of the Bengaline, and kid slippers with buckles. **Fig. b:** this elegant toilette is of apple green French faille, with a front of cream satin richly embroidered and fringed with gold, and the corsage has a pointed plastron to match. The fronts of the low corsage are continued down the skirt in panels, decorated with rows and tasselled loops of Venetian pearl beads; a narrow revers of the silk is turned back on the corsage front. Pearl necklace. Fan of sixteen feathers, white and rose-color. Rose and white aigrette in the hair. Long Suède gloves. Cream silk stockings, and pale green slippers of the faille of the dress.

ACCESSORIES *(4.23.1887, p. 293).* **Fig. a:** the smaller fan is of violet-wood. The end sticks are covered with kid, one of them has a small mirror inlaid, while the other is arranged to slide back, and the space inside is furnished with small scissors, needles, thread and pins. The larger fan has sticks of inlaid wood in two colors, and a narrow cover of white satin with a printed lace design. **Fig. b:** palette-shaped fan of brown silk crêpe, decorated in watercolors. The other fan has gilded sticks, and a cover which represents three lily pads, made of crêped silk gauze, one leaf brown, one yellow, and one red. **Fig. c:** the round hat for spring has a sloping crown of beige and yellow checkered straw, and a high turban brim of darker beige and brown fancy straw. A scarf of beige-colored velvet is curved in a large loop of yellow and brown striped ribbon placed before it. **Fig. d:** the crown of the spring bonnet is of yellow, tulle, covered on the sides with a net-work of jet, which projects in points at the back edges, showing a bar of yellow between. The brim is faced with black velvet, and covered with a wreath of primroses. The front has a high trimming of black lace and primroses, and black lace is carried in folds along the sides. The strings are black lace scarfs.

a   b   c   d

SPRING AND SUMMER WRAPPINGS *(4.30.
1887, pp. 312–313).*
Fig. a: striped grenadine mantle, front (see
fig. f).
Fig. b: cloth jacket.
Fig. c: long morning or travelling cloak, front
(see fig. h).
Fig. d: repped silk mantle.
Fig. e: crêpe de chine mantle.
Fig. f: striped grenadine mantle, back (see
fig. a).
Fig. g: plain and beaded grenadine mantle.
Fig. h: long morning or travelling cloak, back
(see fig. c).

e   *f*   *g*   *h*

a   *b*   *c*

d

YACHTING AND TENNIS GOWNS *(7.30.1887, p. 533)*. These models represent the square-fronted jackets, the belted corsage, amply draped skirts, and many other features in favor this season. (Designs by the courtesy of the Messrs. Redfern.) **Fig. a:** this youthful gown has a red serge Eton jacket, a white cloth waistcoat with gilt cord and buttons, and a navy blue serge skirt with white cloth panels and a short apron. Gilt anchors of cord are on the white cuffs of the red jacket, and anchors trim the skirt on the hips and at the foot. The red straw hat has a white ribbon band and bow. **Fig. b:** this pretty dress for either tennis or yachting is of blue and white striped serge or flannel, with a blouse-waist of dark blue India silk or surah. The jacket is of simple sacque shape, quite short in behind, pointed in front, opening from the collar down. The lower skirt has wide pleats, and the apron is deep and pointed. White cloth sailor hat with blue ribbon band. **Fig. c:** this costume has a blue jacket, skirt and cap, decorated with red anchors. The draped bodice is of washing silk or of white wool, with a gilt belt and gilt buttons. The jacket is short and adjusted behind, but falls open in front in square tabs; it is lined throughout with red silk which shows at the top when turned back. **Fig. d:** this gown is of white wool, with surplice belted waist and plastron, belt, sash, and borders of blue and white striped wool or of washing silk.

a   b

TRAVELLING AND HOME TOILETTES
(10.15.1887, cover). **Fig. a:** this graceful house dress is of supple wool of chamois ground with cherry-colored silk stripes, trimmed with bright green velvet ribbon. The round lower skirt falls in large loose folds that are not held as pleats. The second skirt forms a pointed apron caught up by velvet ribbon loops on one side to show a panel of rows of velvet, and curved as a small panier on the other side; below this panier the apron and the back drapery are caught together by velvet ribbon bands finished with bows. Standing collar of velvet. A ribbon star held by a diamond in the hair. **Fig. b:** this graceful cloak for autumn journeys is of silver gray vigogne, trimmed with darker gray passementerie and dull red velvet. It is lined throughout with supple silk of a lighter shade of gray. The passementerie brings in the back of the cape, and forms a Greek square in the corner of the point. Red velvet revers in front and up the back of the skirt. Collar of red velvet. Torsade of passementerie at the throat and hanging behind. Toque of red velvet, trimmed with gray Bengaline and dark gray cocks' plumes. Half-high shoes and gray stockings. Red Normandy parasol, with the handle covered with light leather.

a *b*

VISITING TOILETTES (*12.24.1887, p. 889*).
Fig. a: visiting costume of pearl gray cloth, trimmed with gold embroidery and cut-work done on the cloth, and chinchilla fur. The round skirt is very plain, and is bordered with chinchilla. The vest is of pearl gray China crape, pleated below and gathered above; a band of the embroidery with a slight edge of fur is down each side to the vest, and crosses it on the bust and at the end. Other bands of embroidery come out from under the arms on the gasque only, and still others form a collar and cuffs. Hat of red felt, trimmed with red velvet, red feather, and gray ribbon. Mastic-colored Suède gloves. **Fig. b:** rich cloak of golden brown silk, a soft thick gros grain, combined with ciselé velvet that has large brown figures on a pale blue satin ground. The fur trimming is natural beaver. This cloak, which opens slightly at the foot in front to show a pleating of brocade, is of the visite-redingote shape. The fronts and the skirt gathered at the top are of the brown silk; the side panels and large visite sleeves are of the velvet. A passementerie ornament trims the back. Brown felt hat turned up high in front and trimmed with blue China crape and blue and brown feathers. The small muff is of the brown silk, edged with the velvet, and trimmed with a bow of brown ribbon.

a   *b*

RECEPTION AND EVENING TOILETTES
(4.7.1888, p. 221). **Fig. a:** this toilette for the
hostess at an afternoon reception is a trained
princesse dress of sapphire blue velvet opening over pale pink faille trimmed with blonde
lace and gold embroidery. The round skirt
of pink faille is trimmed quite near the front
with a panel of gold embroidery, and then
draped with lace shirred to the belt and falling
in shell or jabot fashion to the foot on the
left side. The pink silk bodice is plain, and
is draped in blouse style with lace, then

finished at the neck with a double Pierrot collar pointed low about the throat. Velvet slippers and pink silk stockings. **Fig. b:** this pretty
dress for balls and evening receptions has a
pleated skirt of French faille of the pink shade
known as Rose Dubarry, nearly covered by
a full long drapery of pink tulle dotted with
black and edged with a flounce of the tulle
scalloped with black. Bows of black velvet
ribbon with gold-pointed ends drape the skirt
and trim the waist in front, on the shoulders,
and on the velvet girdle. The low corsage is

of faille draped with tulle at the top, while
the sides and back are covered with a little
Spanish jacket of black velvet trimmed with
gold embroidery. Pale flesh pink gloves of
undressed kid. Coiffure somewhat in the
Empire style, with Greek bandeaux of gold
and a high panache of pink ostrich tips. Pink
ostrich gauze fan painted with pansies in black
and yellow. Pink silk stockings. Pink silk
slipper with black velvet bows.

a

b

BRIDAL AND TRAVELLING DRESSES
(9.29.1888, cover). **Fig. a:** this Parisian model
for a wedding is made of ivory satin, draped
with Brussels lace and trimmed with orange
blossoms. The long plain train is mounted
above the pointed back forms of the corsage,
the sides are flat in redingote style, and the
front has full drapery of lace from head to
foot. The left side of the lace is concealed
by draped ribbon and long-looped flat bows.

Long cordon of orange blossoms on the sides
of the skirt. Long tulle veil held by a cluster
of orange blossoms just above the Pompadour
roll of hair. White undressed kid gloves. White
slippers and white silk stockings. Ivory-bound
prayer-book. **Fig. b:** this French model for
a travelling dress is well suited for the going
away gown of a bride during autumn months.
It is composed of silver gray camel's-hair
combined with velvet of a darker shade, and

finished with an Empire sash of gray soft-
finished silk which passes three times around
the waist and falls low in front, where it is
completed by passementerie tassels. Gray felt
hat with shaded long ostrich plume, worn with
low braided Catogan coiffure tied with a ribbon bow. Light gray Suède gloves. Seal
leather bag with old-silver mountings.

a

b

c

d

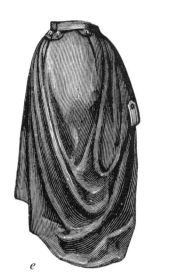

e

f

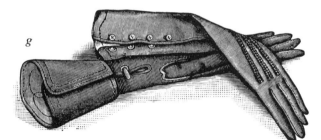

g

h

RIDING COSTUMES *(4.14.1888, p. 245).*
Three kinds of riding-habits are made by fashionable tailors, those for wearing in Central Park being different from those intended for the hunt, and the latter entirely distinct from the simpler habits worn in the summer in the country. English styles are closely copied in all kinds of habits, the skirt being made short and scant, the bodice extremely plain, and the trousers long enough to strap under the feet, or else short knee-breeches are used with top-boots. **Fig. a:** English riding-habit. **Fig. b:** trousers for riding-habit. **Fig. c:** riding-corset, back and front.

RIDING COSTUMES *(5.25.1889, p. 384).*
Fig. d: English riding-habit.
Fig. e: skirt of riding-habit.
Fig. f: inner view of basque of riding-habit.
Fig. g: riding gloves.
Fig. h: collar pins for riding-habits.
Fig. i: walking and travelling shoes and riding boot.

i

MOURNING CLOTHES *(5.10.1888, p. 324).*
Fig. a: braided camel's-hair costume.
Fig. b: Henrietta cloth and crape costume.
Fig. c: mourning handkerchiefs.
Fig. d: gauze bonnet.
Fig. e: English crape walking hat.
Fig. f: English crape bonnet.
Fig. g: young lady's sling-sleeved wrap.
Fig. h: crape-trimmed mantle for elderly lady.

d

e

f

g

h

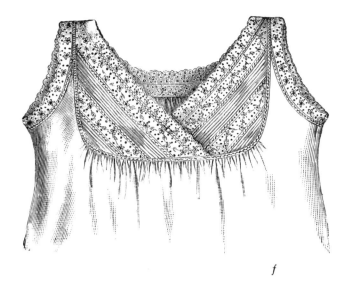

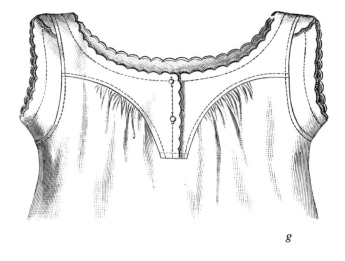

f

g

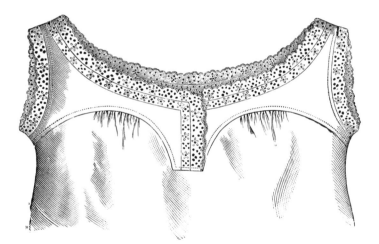

e

d

a

LINGERIE *(8.25.1888, p. 561).*

Fig. a: combing mantle.
Fig. b: piqué breakfast jacket.
Fig. c: cashmere breakfast jacket.
Fig. d: linen collar and cuff.
Fig. e: yoke chemise for stout lady.
Fig. f: chemise with plastron yoke.
Fig. g: chemise with yoke.
Fig. h: cambric drawers.
Fig. i: muslin drawers.
Fig. j: flannel drawers.

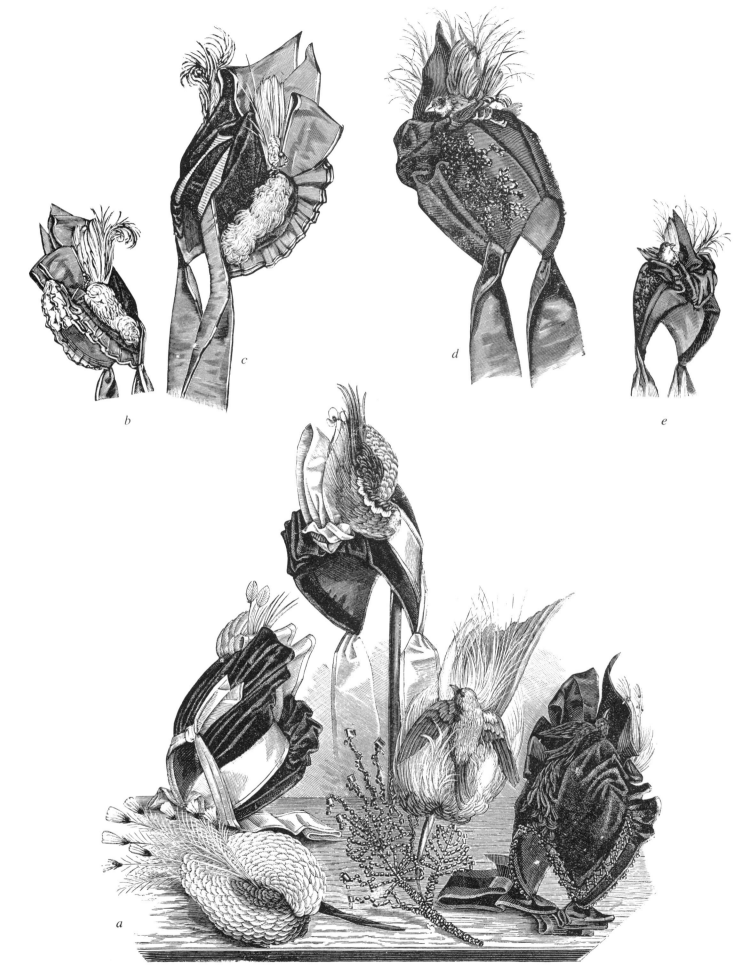

f

g

WINTER BONNETS AND TRIMMINGS
(10.27.1888, p. 713). **Fig. a:** two views of a dark green velvet bonnet are given in the illustration. The small capote frame has a coronet, front on which the velvet is laid smoothly at the sides and puffed at the top. The velvet is formed into close folds on the back of the crown, which are drawn up and project beyond the edge of the frame at the top. A band of pea green ribbon is stretched around the side. A black and red bonnet is shown at the right of the cut. The black velvet of which it is made is puffed at the top of the crown and forms a frill on the brim. A roll of red tulle under a jet net-work is inside the brim, and a similar roll of red tulle surrounds the crown outside. A high bow of black and red striped ribbon, a red aigrette, and a black bird are the ornaments. Three aigrettes are also shown in the illustration, two of them of variously tinted and mounted fancy feathers, and the third consisting of a spray of skeleton leaves made of jet beads.

BODICES, COLLAR AND BONNETS *(12.18. 1888, p. 852).* **Fig. b:** velvet and ribbon bonnet, front. **Fig. c:** velvet and ribbon bonnet, back. **Fig. d:** cloth costume bonnet, back. **Fig. e:** cloth costume bonnet, front. **Fig. f:** frilled bands of gold-dotted red tulle are used to form this collar and jabot. **Fig. g:** this blue jersey has a vest, collar and cuffs embroidered with metallic thread in several tints. **Fig. h:** copper-colored jersey with wide-open rounded fronts filled in with a pleated vest that is crossed by a girdle at the waist. A thick plaited silk and metal cord finishes all the edges.

h

a   b

HOUSE GOWNS *(2.2.1889, p. 76)*. **Fig. a:** this graceful gown for receptions is of Nile green China crape, with a sash of black watered ribbon and garniture of pink blossoms. The round skirt is of green faille or satin, draped with a double-ruffled tablier of green gauze, and finished at the foot with a gauze flounce; narrow green ribbon is gathered at the head of these ruffles and also borders them. The sides and back of the skirt are of the figured China crape, falling in natural folds, and gathered or pleated at the top. The low square corsage is covered by shirred gauze along the top and on the shoulders, from whence it falls, draping the bust and disapppearing under a

corselet of China crape which crosses to the right side and fastens under a bouquet of blossoms. A shoulder knot of the gauze is over the right arm, and an epaulette of flowers on the left. The coiffure is a flower aigrette, and the fan, repeating the colors of the accessories of the gown, is made of rose-pink gauze mounted on black sticks. Long mastic Suède gloves. Green slippers and stockings. **Fig. b:** this Parisian toilette is of black silk brocaded with clusters of pink barley spikes and trimmed with pink pleatings and corselet of silk crêpon. The round skirt is of the brocade in full natural folds, with a slightly draped tablier bordered on each side with shell-

pleating of double rows of the pink crêpon; a flounce of crêpon is pleated across the foot. A large sash of the crêpon hangs low in the back, and is not connected with the wide girdle that crosses the front of the waist. The brocade is gathered full at the throat and disappears under the girdle; two full shell-pleatings of crêpon extend from the collar to the girdle, and the collar is of the pink crêpon in pleats passing around the neck. The easy coat sleeves are trimmed around the armholes with pink folds, and have pink pleating turned back from the wrists.

LADIES' CLASS AT THE FENCER'S CLUB *(4.6.1889, cover)*. Some two years ago a number of ladies who had witnessed the grace and dexterity of their male friends, in an exhibition of fencing given by the Fencers' Club thought they also would be benefited by such exercise. In practicing, the ladies wear an ordinary tennis skirt and flat-soled shoes, no corset, an easy-fitting blouse or jersey. A wire mask protects the face, a padded buckskin *plastron* is worn over the chest, and a buckskin gauntlet saves the hand from any chance scratches or thrusts.

a   *b*

SPRING TOILETTES *(2.16.1889, p. 112).*
Early models furnished by the courtesy of
Messrs. Lord and Taylor. Among these are
shown modifications of the round Empire
waist with its great sash and full skirt, of the
Directoire redingote with its slender effect,
and also of the long over-skirt which young
ladies are not willing to abandon entirely.
Fig. a: this youthful-looking costume of plaid
wool either rosewood and white, metallic blue
and cream, or green with beige, is also a good
model for cashmeres and other plain-surfaced
wool fabrics. Straw Empire hat with ribbon
to match the dress. **Fig. b:** this costume of
bordered wool has a long over-skirt, with the
back attached to the back of the waist, while
the front of the waist is separate. The border
forms the trimming for the skirt, drapery, and
revers. Aureole hat of straw, with gathered
surah facing the brim and rose clusters on
the crown. **Fig. c:** the Directoire redingote is
made of réséda twilled wool, on which is a
large broche Persian design wrought in many
soft colors. The long vest, the wide sash, and
the short broad revers are fashionable features
of new dresses, and the back and sides are
in princesse breadths, continuous from neck
to foot. The Directoire hat is of straw the
color of the dress, with bow inside the brim,
and darker ostrich plumes nodding over the
front. **Fig. d:** this dress of Empire green serge
with broché cream figures on the front breadth
and as a border for trimming is a compromise
between the extreme styles of the Empire and
of the Directory. The waist is slightly pointed
in front and is round behind—a fashion preferred by those who find the sash and short waists
unbecoming. The bonnet has soft puffs of silk
for the crown, with a velvet coronet and
cocks' feather trimming.

c   d

a   *b*   *c*   *d*   *e*   *f*

g   h i   j   k   l

SPRING AND SUMMER WRAPPINGS
(4.20.1889, pp. 288–289).
Fig. a: long cloak for girl from 11 to 13 years old.
Fig. b: bordered wool cloak.
Fig. c: lace fichu-wrap, back (see fig g).
Fig. d: black silk paletot.
Fig. e: frock for girl from 8 to 10 years.
Fig. f: tailor jacket with revers.
Fig. g: lace fichu-wrap, front (see fig. c).
Fig. h: Directoire cape with hood, front (see fig. l).
Fig. i: frock for girl from 6 to 8 years old.
Fig. j: braided visite.
Fig. k: frock for boy from 2 to 4 years old.
Fig. l: Directoire cape with hood, back (see fig. h).

a

b

OUT-DOOR TOILETTES *(10.26.1889, cover).* **Fig. a:** this graceful long cloak is a French model made of faced cloth of the new dark red, called Buffalo red, trimmed with black cord passementerie. Buffalo felt hat trimmed with black velvet and black ostrich feathers. Red stockings and black shoes. Tan-colored kid gloves and black umbrella. **Fig. b:** the pretty visiting dress is made of striped changeable silk (rose, green, and brown) trimmed with black velvet bands and van-dykes of white Irish guipure lace. The round skirt is nearly flat in front, with a little fullness taken up on each hip to give a slight *mouvement,* as the French say, and break the otherwise too uniform lines.

THE SURPRISE DRESS—OPEN AND CLOSED (*11.9.1889, cover*). One of the novelties of the season is the surprise dress, which combines a street costume and house gown so perfectly that a lady can go out in a plain walking or travelling dress which by a simple manipulation can be changed into quite a gay house gown suitable for luncheon or visiting. The model is of black silk, opening on pale old-rose embroidered in black. It is taken up on the side by means of a button and loop cleverly concealed in a fold.

h   i   k   l

EVENING TOILETTES *(1.18.1890, pp. 48–49)*.

Fig. a: dinner dress.
Fig. b: modern classical gown.
Fig. c: ball dress with draped bodice.
Fig. d: reception dress with short train.
Fig. e: black velvet evening gown.
Fig. f: young lady's dancing dress.
Fig. g: ball dress of mousseline de soie and brocade.
Fig. h: gown with velvet bodice and train.
Fig. i: debutante's dress.
Fig. j: reception toilette.
Fig. k: white bengaline dress.
Fig. l: short evening dress.

SPRING AND SUMMER GOWNS (*3.1.1890, p. 164*). **Fig. a:** this model is a graceful gown of India silk, with black ground strewn with pink and yellow blossoms. The full bodice without darts or side forms is made over a fitted lining and is fastened on the right side under a jabot of black lisse. Black satin ribbon edges the bodice, and drops in loops in front. Large straw hat trimmed with pink ribbon and pink and cream-colored blossoms. **Fig. b:** the gown on this figure has the bordered skirt now made for summer wool or gingham dresses. In the dress illustrated the skirt is of lavender wool, widely bordered with cream-white canvas that is striped with darker lavender and black. Wide-brimmed straw hat, trimmed with

lavender ribbon and pink blossoms. **Fig. c:** this tailor gown of réséda cloth shown next is a Parisian adaptation of the straight English skirt and habit-basque. The habit-basque opens on a collar and chemisette of white linen or cloth, with a sailor-knotted scarf of emerald green silk. Black straw hat with green plumes. **Fig. d:** another bordered gown, with a border half the depth of the skirt, is of pale blue wool, with écru bands, finished at the foot with two black bengaline stripes. Wide point de Gênes lace forms cuffs on the sleeves and a cravat. Pale blue bengaline ribbon is used for the belt, sash, and bows. Yellow straw hat, trimmed with lace and fine flowers.

a   *b*   *c*   *d*   *e*   *f*

h   j   k   l

AUTUMN AND WINTER WRAPPINGS
(10.18.1890, pp. 812–813).
Fig. a: frock for girl from 5 to 7 years old.
Fig. b: long cloak with velvet sleeves, back (see fig. k).
Fig. c: coat for girl from 2 to 4 years old.
Fig. d: velvet mantle.
Fig. e: Louis XIII jacket.
Fig. f: fur-trimmed cloak.
Fig. g: repped silk jacket with feather trimming, back (see fig. j).
Fig. h: fur-trimmed cloak, back (see fig. f).
Fig. i: braided jacket.
Fig. j: repped silk jacket with feather trimming, front (see fig. g).
Fig. k: long cloak with velvet sleeves, front (see fig. b).
Fig. l: coat for girl from 7 to 9 years old.

WINTER JACKETS AND CLOAKS *(12.20.1890, p. 1009).* The dressy coat of three-quarters length, with cross seams on the hips and flap pockets, is of gray cloth trimmed with black chenille, and oxidized silver cord set on in a large curled design. The garment closes in the middle of the front under the boa of black ostrich feathers. The chenille and silver trimming is on the deep cuffs and down the back of the skirt. The buttons are of the cloth set in silver rims. The hat worn with this coat is of gray felt, with soft beaver trim, much crinkled in front, with tips of black ostrich and silver galloon as trimming. The long cloak with a cape has semi-fitting fronts and closely fitted back, with the fullness of the skirt gathered to the middle forms of the back instead of being pleated in the usual way. The fabric is camel's-hair of large diagonal weaving, in a new shade of gray-blue. A bor-der around the entire garment is of natural gray ostrich feathers, and to this is added, on the cape, a blue passementerie fringe. The large black hat has a brim of felt, with a black velvet crown in soft large folds, edged with small curling ostrich tips. A cluster of tips is set high on the back of the crown. A band of black velvet crosses the back, and supports a cluster of red roses that rest on the hair.

SUMMER BONNETS AND HATS *(6.15.1889, p. 448)*. **Fig. a:** a light straw bonnet with a coronet front filled in with a ruche and small blossoms, high loops of changeable pink and gold ribbon surmounting the whole. **Fig. b:** bonnet of Neapolitan and fancy straw, having a peaked front trimmed with flowers and Empire green ribbon loops, with smaller ribbon bows strapped to the sides. **Fig. c:** an Empire hat of gray-green scalloped straw. A single rose with foliage rests against the soft tulle facing in the brim; outside are a few loops of striped ribbon, and long and short ostrich plumes shading from dark green to white. **Fig. d:** a girlish hat in saucer shape, fitted to the head by a band inside which is covered with ribbon and ornamented with a bow. A flat bow of ribbon on the centre of the crown and flowing streamers behind complete the hat. **Fig. e:** a wide-brimmed shade hat for a young girl of light-colored straw, with a cluster of field flowers fastened by loops of a narrow ribbon on one side, and a vine from it encircling the brim.

IV

HOURGLASS FIGURE

❧ 1891-1898 ❧

The bustled book lingered, if only vestigially, into the 1890s (Evening Toilettes, pp. 228–229, 236–237). By 1893 a form often referred to as the "hourglass" figure had taken shape. Ballooning sleeve and widening skirts helped to make an already tightly corseted waist seem even smaller, giving the silhouette the appearance of two separate round masses joined in the middle (Autumn and Winter Costumes, pp. 260–261; Paris Spring Toilette, p. 270; French Promenade Costume, p. 281).

Costumes by French designers, particularly those by Worth, dominated the pages of *Harper's Bazar*. Made of velvets, satins and lush silks, richly embroidered and lavishly trimmed in fanciful combinations, these costumes held a great appeal to moneyed Americans (Worth Cloak, p. 248; Evening Gowns, pp. 249, 264; Calling Costume, p. 282; Reception Gown, p. 286). Their undisputed opulence provided a great showcase for wealth. But at the same time interest developed in simpler and even quite masculine-looking tailored suits (Outing Gowns, p. 253). The American girl, as depicted by Charles Dana Gibson, elevated the combination of skirt and shirtwaist into the realm of fashion. Now even women who were forced to work for a living had an opportunity to enter the elite world of chic (Waists, pp. 267; Summer Costumes, p. 287). The designs for commencement dresses indicate that higher education for women had increased to a point that warranted a special costume (Graduates' Commencement Gowns, p. 252). "Suggestions for making Commencement dresses are asked of the BAZAR from all over the country by young girls who are soon to graduate from high-school, seminary, or college" (April 15, 1893).

Women continued to make their greatest strides by becoming active—yet fashionable—in many previously barred sports such as hunting, golfing, driving and mountain climbing (Mountain Dresses, p. 230; Game of Golf, p. 273; Sporting Costumes, p. 280; Hunting Costume, p. 258). During this decade cycling, which had been gaining popular interest and support since the 1860s, became the rage. Coupled with the still existing Victorian sense of modesty, bicycling finally made pants a socially and fashionably acceptable garment for public wear by women. Beginning with Amelia Bloomer in the 1850s, there had been a number of attempts to introduce trousers as fitting and proper apparel for

women. In 1869 some skating costumes with pants were shown (Difference Skating Costumes, p. 13), but this was proposition rather than fact; until the middle of the 1890s costumes with trousers were only accepted for bathing at the beach. Although pants had been designed for riding, they were meant to be concealed under the skirts of the habit (Riding Costume, p. 202).

The French gave their stamp of approval to the new bloomer cycling costume but, unlike the Americans who portrayed women as able participants in sports, they continued to show fashions which focused on the allure of feminine frailty, even in a sporting setting (Bicycle Dress, p. 266; Seaside Toilette, p. 232; Yachting Costume, p. 269).

Underwear, while generally frillier than ever, also showed the impact of this spirit of growing simplicity and liberation; new forward-looking undergarments such as the combinations and bloomers made their appearance. Teagowns, as they grew in popularity, became elaborate showpieces (Tea Gowns, pp. 233, 292). This item had been introduced in the late 1870s as an at-home robe created to allow women a measure of freedom while relaxing with female friends in the afternoon.

By 1896 sleeves had become so large that they began to flop over. At the same time, the next fashion cycle began to take shape, with its accent on the bosom, in the form of exaggerated fullness in the bodice front (Paris Walking Costume, p. 279). In 1897 fashions went into transition. The emphasis on shoulder extension was reduced to a token width provided by a kind of epaulette treatment over slim sleeves with some gathers at the top (Cashmere House Gown, p. 283). Fullness slipped into the bodice, and there was a new "chest-out" look that was to develop into the large "mono-bosom" of the early twentieth century. Other elements of the coming reverse-S silhouette began to enter the scene. Bodices had high necks which were stiffened with boning to keep the head back and the chin out. Skirts were slimmed down to reveal the slow curve of the hips and became longer in the back (Cloth Gown, p. 284; Demi-saison Gowns, p. 288). Without breaking step, fashion went on to bridge two centuries (Paris Model, p. 290).

a   *b*   *c*   *d*   *e*   *f*   *g*   *h*

EVENING AND BALL TOILETTES *(1.24. 1891, pp. 64–65).*

Fig. a: embroidered satin gown.

Fig. b: embroidered crape dress, back (see fig. i).

Fig. c: black satin gown.

Fig. d: China silk gown.

Fig. e: young lady's tulle dress.

Fig. f: spotted tulle gown with feather trimming, front (see fig. l).

Fig. g: velvet gown.

Fig. h: faille gown with feather trimming.

Fig. i: embroidered crape dress, front (see fig. b).

Fig. j: velvet and satin dress.

Fig. k: crêpe de chine dress.

Fig. l: spotted tulle gown with feather trimming, back (see fig. f).

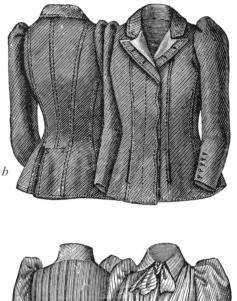

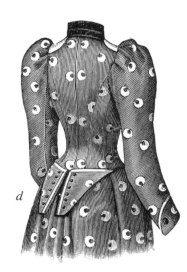

f

g

MOUNTAIN, BOATING AND TENNIS DRESSES *(5.30.1891, p. 425).*
Fig. a: mountain dress.
Fig. b: jacket for mountain dress.
Fig. c: shirt waist for mountain dress.

Fig. d: back of boating dress.
Fig. e: back of tennis dress.
Fig. f: boating dress.
Fig. g: tennis dress.

A SEASIDE TOILETTE *(6.6.1891, cover).*
This charming picture tells its own story.
Summer is come, and the graceful *mondaine*
quits the delights of the town for the invigora-
ting breezes wafted over the sunlit water. It
is afternoon, yet her gown is of the simplest,
fashioned exquisitely by Worth from soft fine
wool of the pale tint of Persian lilacs. The
rich *camail*, or bishop's mantle, is of cream-
colored *molleton*, a soft flannel-like cloth. It
is studded with jet cabochons, and has a yoke
of jetted passementerie, with rain fringe of
jet, and a flaring collar finished with a lace
ruff. The hat, from the Maison Virot, is of
transparent black horse-hair popularly known
here as Neapolitan braid. Rose-colored ribbon is added in erect wired loops at the back,
and long streamers hanging down the waist.
A parasol of white chiffon mousseline completes the toilette.

TEA GOWN FROM WORTH *(12.12.1891, p. 957).* This gown is a masterpiece, unique in design and in materials. It is a long flowing caftan of beige-colored cloth, draped over a velvet gown which fits the slender figure with sheath-like closeness. *Velours frappé* (stamped velvet) with maroon design on lighter ground, is used for the front of the close gown; it is fitted by darts and extends far back on the sides, fastening invisibly on the left. The fronts frame the slight figure with wide revers of white plush; their fulness is narrowly massed on the shoulders, with ends carried thence to the middle of the back, and knotted there above full back breadths that fall in Watteau-like pleats. A high collar has velvet at the back, and is covered in front with white lace extending lower in a pointed plastron. Deep cuffs of lace are on the sleeves.

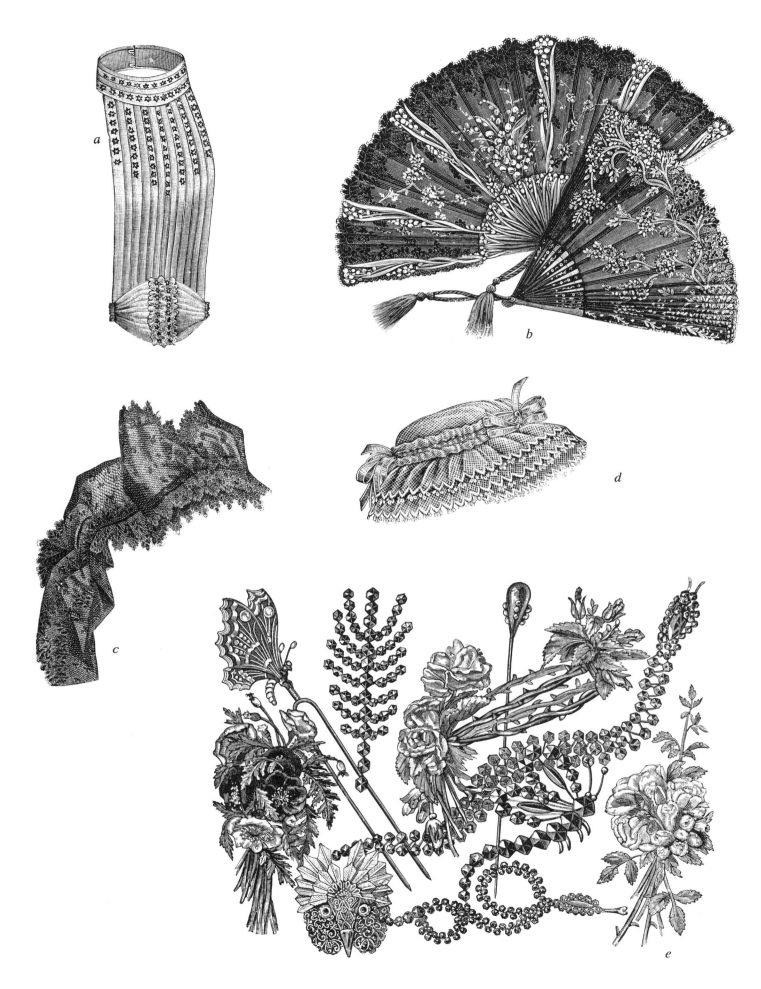

ACCESSORIES *(9.5.1891, p. 680).*
Fig. a: crêpe vest.
Fig. b: evening fans.
Fig. c: cap for aged lady.
Fig. d: breakfast cap.

HAT ORNAMENTS *(5.9.1891, p. 360).*
Fig. e.

ACCESSORIES *(12.26.1891, p. 1025).*
Fig. f: house and walking shoes.
Fig. g: leather belts with metal mountings.

ACCESSORIES *(9.3.1892, p. 721).*
Fig. h: watch-pins, fan-holder, and enamelled
  brooches.
Fig. i: belts and shoe-horn with buttoner.

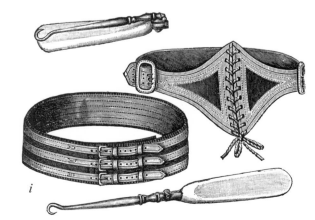

a   *c*   *b*   *d*   *e*   *f*

EVENING TOILETTES *(1.2.1892, pp. 8–9).*
Fig. a: crépon gown.
Fig. b: velvet gown with lace.
Fig. c: brocade and chiffon dress.
Fig. d: peau de soie gown.
Fig. e: bengaline gown with lace.
Fig. f: chiffon gown.
Fig. g: gown with lace and feather trimming (see fig. j).
Fig. h: fur-trimmed satin gown.
Fig. i: peau de soie gown with spangled chiffon.
Fig. j: gown with lace and feather trimming (see fig. g).

g   h   i   j

WORTH'S SEAMLESS DRESS *(2.20.1892, cover)*. Seamless corsages have found such favor that a seamless dress has been produced by Worth's creative brain. This dress of elastic wool, as ladies' cloth or crépon, drawn smoothly over a fitted waist lining of silk, and covering a bell-shaped skirt of silk. Cutting the cloth bias facilitates matters in these dresses, as it then clings more closely when stretched around the waist, and also furnishes greater fulness in the skirt. Seams that are absolutely necessary are concealed by trimming, and the dress is fastened invisibly, usually on the left side. The dress illustrated gives the effect of a princesse back, with round waist front. Blue cloth is the material used, with sleeves and panel of narrow bias folds applied on a maize yellow ground. The yellow contrast, now so fashionable with blue, is further given in open gold passementerie. Later in the season the fur band can be replaced by a fine ruche of gold ribbon. Changeable taffeta silks are used by French modistes for the waist and skirt lining of wool dresses, with a pinked balayeuse of the gay silk at the foot.

DUST CLOAKS FROM WORTH (*4.9.1892, cover*). A travelling cloak large enough to envelop the dress beneath is of satin merveilleux with glossy surface that repels dust. It is shot in copper shades, and the light lining is of fancy surah. The second protective outfit has a long jacket with a skirt to match made of Silesienne, a ribbed fabric of light weight and self-colored. The peculiar feature of the jacket is a Watteau fold down the front as well as the back.

BONNETS AND PARASOLS *(4.23.1892, p. 341).*

Fig. a: jet bonnet.
Fig. b: jet bonnet.
Fig. c: jet bonnet frame.
Fig. d: jet bonnet frame.
Fig. e: hat for girl from 4 to 6 years old.
Fig. f: girl's sailor hat.
Fig. g: breakfast cap.
Fig. h: parasols.

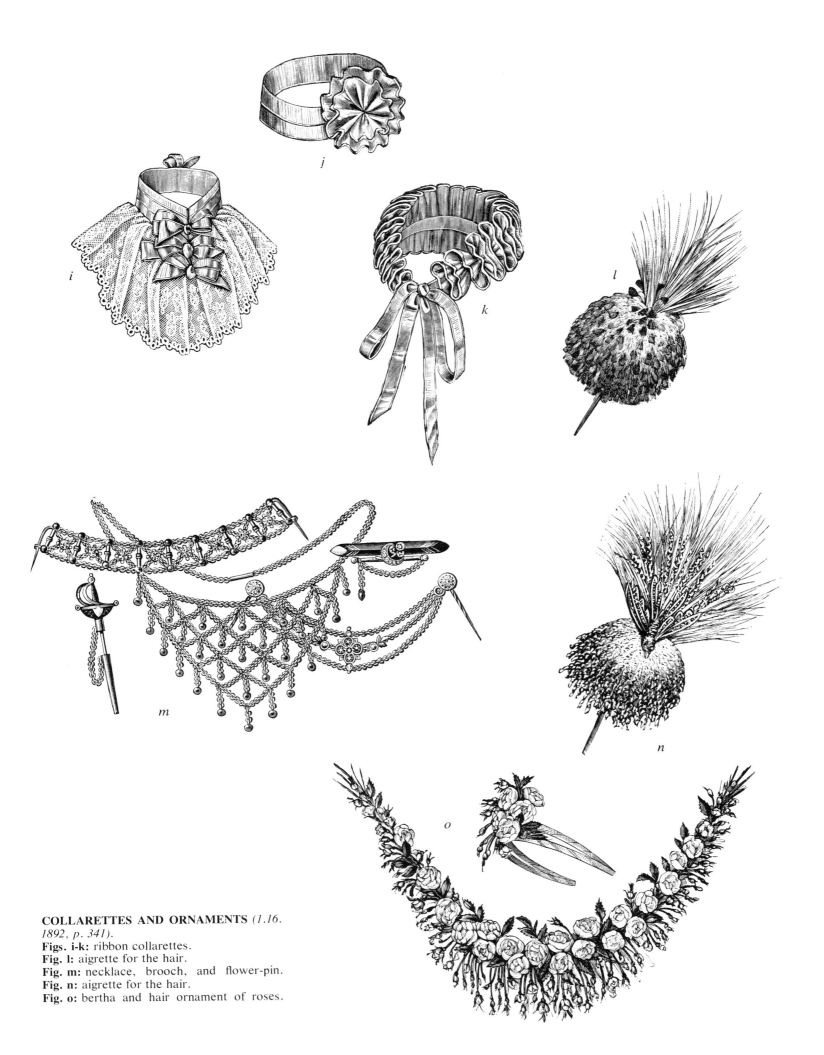

COLLARETTES AND ORNAMENTS *(1.16.
1892, p. 341).*
Figs. i-k: ribbon collarettes.
Fig. l: aigrette for the hair.
Fig. m: necklace, brooch, and flower-pin.
Fig. n: aigrette for the hair.
Fig. o: bertha and hair ornament of roses.

e d b   f   g c a   h

CHILDREN'S AND INFANTS' WEAR
(5.14.1892, p. 393).
Fig. a: baby's long cloak.
Fig. b: baby's wrapper, cap and bib.

Fig. c: baby's frock with guimpe.
Fig. d: frock for girl from 7 to 9 years old.
Fig. e: little boy's jacket.
Fig. f: little girl's jacket.

Fig. g: frock for girl from 1 to 3 years old.
Fig. h: little girl's cloak and bonnet.

a   b   c

WEDDING AND RECEPTION TOILETTES
(3.4.1893, p. 173). **Fig. a:** white peau de soie is the material of this bridal gown, which is made with a full-trained untrimmed skirt, and a short seamless bodice that is draped with lace on the front, and has a lace jabot carried diagonally across. The tulle veil, which is hemmed at the edge, is fastened on with orange blossoms, and a small cluster of the flowers ornaments the corsage. **Fig. b:** a reception gown for a wedding guest is of gray bengaline with yellow ribbon. The corsage is draped, and the guimpe on which it opens, together with the lower part of the sleeves is embroidered in gold. The collar, the belt with long bow, and the bows which stud the front of the skirt are of yellow velvet ribbon. **Fig. c:** another reception gown is of green faille. The skirt opens on a narrow panel of shot rose and green velvet. The bodice has a low cut round seamless back, while the front is cut like a short open jacket, and inside are a guimpe and vest of yellow; a cape collar rolls from the velvet guimpe; the edges are bordered with silk folds.

a   *b*   *c*   *d*

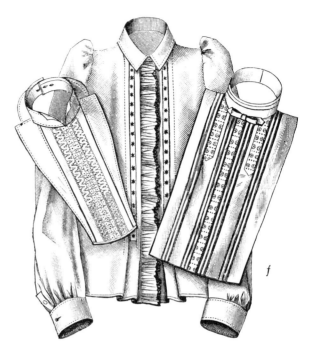

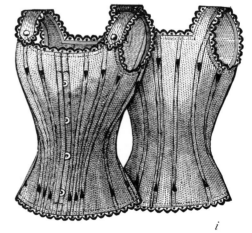

BATHING COSTUMES, SHOES AND SHIRTS. *(6.18.1892, p. 492).*
Fig. a: bathing suit and cap.
Fig. b: bath cloak.
Fig. c: bathing suit and cap.
Fig. d: bathing suit for girl from 6 to 8 years
    old.
Fig. e: travelling and walking shoes.
Fig. f: shirt waist and chemisettes.

LINGERIE *(4.30.1892, p. 360).*
Fig. g: lady's combination garment.
Fig. h: lady's combination garment, back.
Fig. i: négligé corset of jersey webbing.
Fig. j: nightcap or dusting cap.

UNDERGARMENTS AND ACCESSORIES
(7.11.1892, p. 572).
Fig. a: breakfast caps.
Fig. b: corset.
Fig. c: summer hosiery.
Fig. d: ladies' collars and cuffs.
Fig. e: frocks for girls from 2 to 5 years old.
Fig. f: handkerchiefs.
Fig. g: chemise with Valenciennes lace and chemise with plastron.
Fig. h: drawers with yoke band and drawers

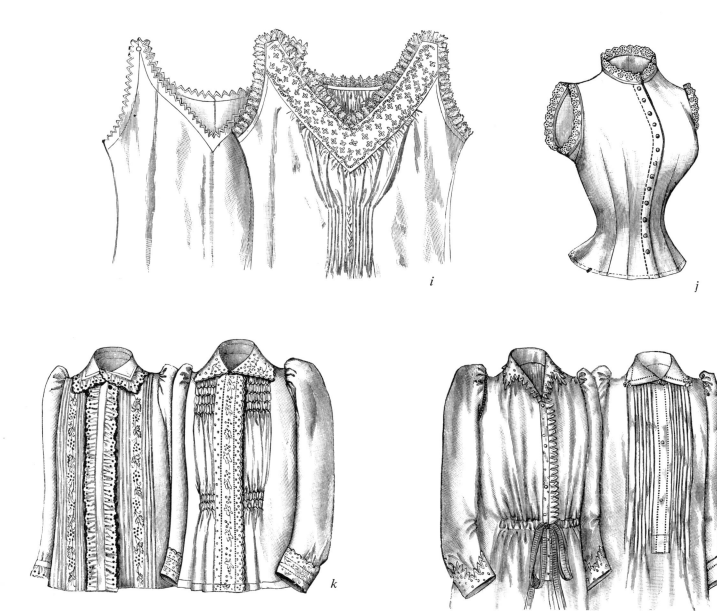

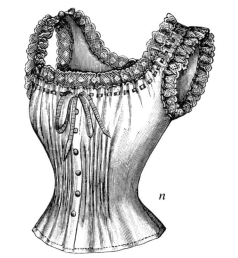

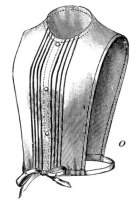

with side fastening.

Fig. i: French chemise and chemise tucked at the waist.

Fig. j: high corset cover.

Fig. k: dressing sacque with tucked front and dressing sacque with shirred front.

Fig. l: night-gown with shirred front and night-gown with tucked front.

Fig. m: trimmings for drawers.

Fig. n: corset cover without side forms.

Fig. o: chemisette.

A WORTH CLOAK SEEN IN THE LOUVRE *(3.4.1893, cover).* This cloak is a recent creation which is given character by its great simplicity of form and the arrangement of its decorations. In ensemble it recalls the styles of old Egyptian costumes, and for this reason the artist has not feared to commit the anachronism of placing the elegent woman who wears it beside the sculptured sphinx in the Musée du Louvre. It is made of fine mastic wool. Two bands of pearl-gray velvet forming scarfs on each shoulder start at the waist in front, and extend just underneath the shoulder-blades in the back. This velvet is embroidered with many rows of jet beads and cabochons. Below the scarf numberless threads of jet fringe fall in festoons on the skirt, and return to be attached in the back. The large sleeves, very bouffant on the shoulders, are pleated below on flaring sleeves of wool widely bordered with silken Persian. The high collar, also of Persian, has turned-over points in front, and very effective revers are added below. Below the revers is a very large ornament of jet, and a pendant of jet butterflies completes this superb cloak. The little capote is of gold braid surrounded by black lace gathered all around. A large dragon-fly with wings of blue and gold is its charming ornament.

AN EVENING GOWN FROM WORTH AND COIFFURE FROM LENTHÉRIC OF PARIS
(4.15.1893, cover). This elegant ball gown of *ciel*-blue damask has a distinctive style given by its rich trimming of embroidered lace and pearls. A charming design of pink chrysanthemum petals is brocaded on delicate blue ground. The corsage is pointed in front, and is trimmed all around the low neck with white tulle and lace gracefully festooned. A double garland of pearls mounted on tulle with crystal pendants starts on the bust and curves to the right at the waist, where it is fastened by clasps in the form of St. Jacques shells. The damask skirt has similar garlands of pearls and crystal festooned diagonally across the front above a flounce of embroidered lace, which drops down the left to join the side of the damask train. At the foot of the skirt, which is gored in umbrella shape, a deep flounce of embroidered lace is added under a ruche of tulle. The hair is parted in the middle and drawn back in large waves to a high coil, and is ornamented with twists of pearls.

a   *b*   *c*   *d*   *e*   *f*   *g*

SPRING AND SUMMER WRAPPINGS
(Spring supplement. 1893, pp. 246–247).
Fig. a: jacket with collarette.
Fig. b: cape with draped collarette.
Fig. c: suit for boy from 5 to 7 years old.
Fig. d: dust or travelling cloak.
Fig. e: driving cloak.
Fig. f: lace Empire jacket.
Fig. g: coat for girl from 3 to 5 years old.
Fig. h: jacket with stole collarette.
Fig. i: cape with braided yoke.
Fig. j: black silk jacket.
Fig. k: frock and jacket for girl from 7 to 9
 years old.

i   *j*   *k*

GRADUATES' COMMENCEMENT GOWNS
(4.15.1893, p. 301). **Fig. a:** a doucet model for simple frocks of the graduates at a fashionable boarding-school is made of such costly fabrics as the new crinkled silk crape, with front of bodice and trimming of white satin with pin-dotted spangled brocading. **Fig. b:** a gown of white China silk for evening commencements, trimmed on waist, corsage, and sleeves with bias ruffles of the same. **Fig. c:** a pretty gown of white surah satin powdered with rings like spangles has a full front of accordion-pleated silk muslin under lengthwise bands of white satin ribbon edged with opalescent beads. **Fig. d:** a gown of pin-dotted Swiss muslin with the Marie Antoinette fichu so becoming to slender figures, is the model chosen by another class of boarding-school graduates. **Fig. e:** a simple dress for high-school graduates of sweet sixteen may be made of dotted Swiss muslin, of plain nainsook, or of China silk.

OUTING GOWNS *(6.24.1893, p. 509)*. Some outing gowns for yachting, boating, and tennis are from models furnished by the courtesy of Messrs. Redfern. Duck, sacking and serge are the materials. The familiar jackets and blazers with shirt waist or waistcoat prevail. The skirts of these dresses are about four yards wide, with gored front and side breadths and full back, or else they have a single seam, that in the back, and are circular in shape. Large sleeves and wide collars like capes give a new finish to gowns made last year. **Fig. a:** a blazer suit pretty for either land or sea is of white serge with rows of tubular braid, or merely a finish of stitching. **Fig. b:** for a patriotic yachtswoman is a gown of red, white and blue serge that may serve for a Fourth of July dinner dress at sea. **Fig. c:** a tennis gown of white hop-sacking is trimmed with bias folds of ombré surah in which red prevails. **Fig. d:** a white duck dress for tennis or for hot days at sea is braided with navy blue, and widely bound with blue dungaree. **Fig. e:** the golf cloak is a long cape of soft thick wool provided with straps inside that encircle the figure and hold the cape securely when it is thrown back on the shoulders. This garment is in favor as a steamer wrap and for long journeys by rail.

a

b

c

INFANTS' AND SMALL CHILDREN'S WEAR *(7.1.1893, p. 552).* For this is the chief beauty of these little garments—that they are made precious by the needle-work that is put into them. The first baby usually has a good deal of this same handiwork about his clothes, and the second generally wears out his elder brother's dainty garments, while poor little number three and his successors must depend upon the sewing machine for the stitching to their frocks. **Fig. a:** white piqué coat. **Fig. b:** cashmere wrapper. **Fig. c:** frock to wear with guimpe.

SMALL BOYS' AND GIRLS' COSTUMES *(7.1.1893, p. 553)*. Up to two years old, and in some cases later, there is no difference made in the costuming of the little boy and the little girl. Indeed, the little girl's frocks undergo few modifications even at a later age. But the small male animal of the human species will probably be made by his doting parents to declare his sex by his garments at as early a period as possible. The first step, of course, is to put him into kilts. **Fig. a:** boy's suit with kilt and reefer jacket. **Fig. b:** boy's white duck suit. **Fig. c:** boy's one-piece pleated frock. **Fig. d:** boy's white piqué frock.

a   *b*   *c*   *d*

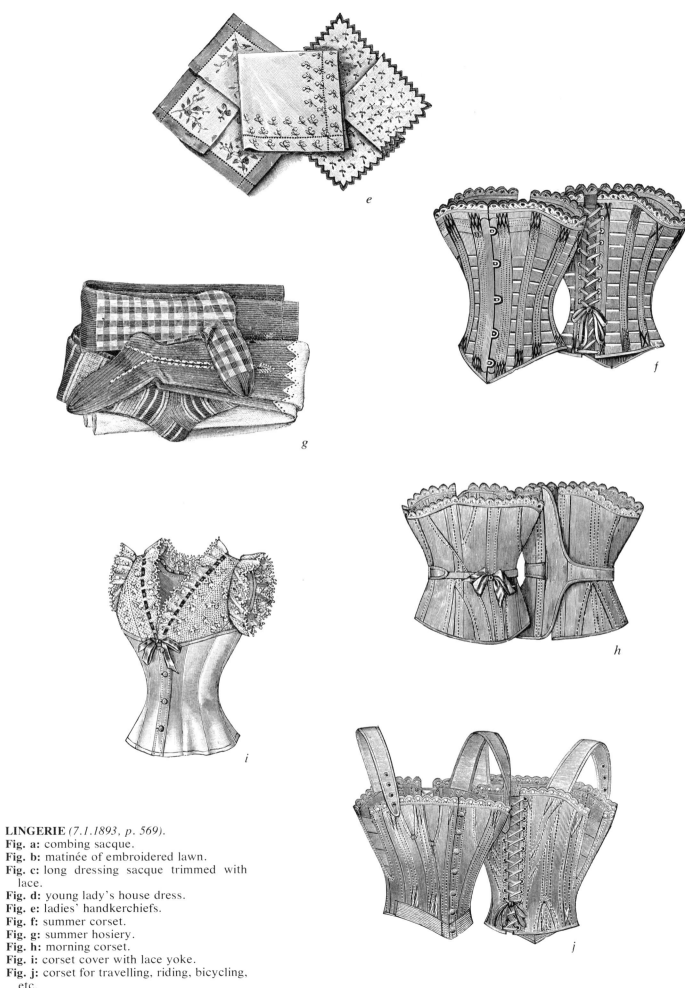

LINGERIE *(7.1.1893, p. 569).*

Fig. a: combing sacque.

Fig. b: matinée of embroidered lawn.

Fig. c: long dressing sacque trimmed with lace.

Fig. d: young lady's house dress.

Fig. e: ladies' handkerchiefs.

Fig. f: summer corset.

Fig. g: summer hosiery.

Fig. h: morning corset.

Fig. i: corset cover with lace yoke.

Fig. j: corset for travelling, riding, bicycling, etc.

LADY'S HUNTING COSTUME AND GENTLEMAN'S SHOOTING SUIT *(8.12. 1893, p. 645).*

a

c

b

PARISIAN WINTER COSTUMES *(11.25. 1893, p. 696).* **Fig. a:** a very *chic* cape with full godet pleats is of light gray cloth braided with darker gray soutache in a design of fern leaves. A collar of gray velvet flares high at the top and extends below to the shoulder-tips, where are seen glimpses of the lining of pinkish lilac satin. Black marten fur borders the entire garment. **Fig. b:** a cloth gown with velvet waist trimmed with fur is in great favor with young women. Russian blue tinged with gray is the new shade for the cloth, and the waist with gigot sleeves is bluish-black velvet. The front of the corsage is covered by a white satin vest with jabot and stock-collar. The velvet fronts are widely faced with sable fur turned back as revers. A felt hat the color of the cloth and pearl-gray gloves complete the costume. **Fig. c:** a picturesque wrap is a cape of black velvet falling in full folds with an inner jacket and high flaring collar of Russian sable. Rich cream-white guipure embroidered with gold covers a collarette of velvet, and forms wide borders on front. A black velvet hat has full trimming of turquoise satin antique with an aigrette and black ostrich tips.

J.CHAPUIS

a   *b*   *c*   *d*   *e*   *f*   *g*

h   *i*   *j*

AUTUMN AND WINTER COSTUMES (*Fall Supplement. 1893, pp. 834–835*).

Fig. a: cloth costume with embroidered vest.

Fig. b: jetted velvet cape with ostrich feather trimming.

Fig. c: coat for girl from 10 to 11 years old.

Fig. d: evening or carriage cloak with velvet cape and fur boa.

Fig. e: braided cloth jacket edged with Persian lamb.

Fig. f: braided tailor gown.

Fig. g: long velvet coat with appliqué embroidery and ostrich trimming.

Fig. h: cloth gown with embroidered velvet.

Fig. i: cloth cape with velvet collar.

Fig. j: seal coat trimmed with Astrakhan, and plaid bouclé wool skirt.

a   *b*   *c*   *d*   *e*

f   g   h   i

EVENING TOILETTES (*12.23.1893, supplement*).

Fig. a: young lady's white satin gown.
Fig. b: velvet and moiré gown.
Fig. c: ball gown of tulle and silk.
Fig. d: broché satin and chiffon gown.
Fig. e: white satin and brocade gown.
Fig. f: clouded moiré gown with lace and crystal trimming.
Fig. g: silk muslin gown with appliqué lace.
Fig. h: faille and velvet gown with embroidery.
Fig. i: broché satin gown with velvet bodice and feather trimming.

EVENING GOWN FROM WORTH, COIFFURE FROM LENTHÉRIC OF PARIS *(3.17.1894, cover)*. This superb gown is of very light *ciel*-blue satin bordered with black fur. It is further enriched with bead embroidery in iris designs. The pointed waist is draped across the bust, and has a jabot falling between branches of embroidery done on the satin. Fur shoulder-straps complete the square décolleté. Short puffed sleeves of dotted mousseline de soie are under a ruffle of beaded satin. The graceful skirt falls in godet pleats, and is trimmed with embroidery and fur. The coiffure is without any ornament, a looped tress at the back extending above the top of the head giving a pretty profile. The fan is of black lace figures appliquéd on tulle.

WORTH EVENING AND CARRIAGE CLOAKS *(4.7.1894, p. 280).* Every accessory of a fashionable woman's toilette is extremely important. Comfort and grace are alike to be considered in the style of wraps she chooses for day or evening. These should sometimes be splendid and harmonious, rich and exquisite in fabric and adornment. Beauty should go beautifully when she drives abroad. The first of these elegant cloaks is used by Parisiennes for the carriage in afternoon drives as well as for an evening wrap. It is made of black satin, trimmed with black marten fur on a part of the cape, and descending like a round boa down the front. The small cape of full pleats is attached to a yoke covered with white guipure mounted on black net. The coiffure, in Empire style, is called Sans Gêne by Lenthéric. It is waved close to the head, and has a large puff and small curls in the back surrounded by strands of pearls. A tiara and aigrette complete the coiffure. A second cloak of black satin is in bell shape, and is embroidered in stripes from the collar to the foot all around. An opening on each side forms a sort of sleeve, which is very long, and is bordered with fur, as is the entire garment. The lining is of pink satin on which white lace is applied. The evening hood from the Maison Virot is of white satin covered with black and white lace trimmed with white satin ribbon.

BICYCLE DRESS *(4.14.1894, cover)*. So much has been said and written upon proper dress for women who ride the wheel that any one who is not a practical cyclist might be pardoned a feeling of bewilderment. Curiously enough, Paris, that stronghold of the conventional dress, has been most fertile in this field. *Faire le bicyclette* is an extremely fashionable sport there, and growing more so. An elegant and attractive form of the French costume is that illustrated. Turkish trousers, long and ample, are made of such fulness that when standing upright the division is obliterated. Very wide at the bottom, they droop deeply upon gaiters of cloth to match. A short double-breasted jacket is buttoned over a vest, collar, and tie. The material is brown velveteen.

SILK WAISTS *(4.28.1894, p. 344).* **Figs. a–c.**

WAISTS *(6.2.1894, p. 437).*
Fig. d: tailor-made shirt waist.
Fig. e: checked silk waist with cherry velvet
  ribbons.
Fig. f: shirt waist with starched front.

G. JOUBARD SC

J. CHAPUIS

A PARIS SUMMER GOWN AND HAT
(*6.9.1894, p. 457*). This graceful gown is a
pretty model for a sultane. It is of the popular
pale beige shade. The corsage has a rather
long basque, that is belted with beige satin
ribbon fastened by a gold buckle in a way
much like in summer gowns. The full front
of the waist is of light yellow accordion-
pleated mousseline de soie. Gracefully draped

revers and the godet basque are covered
smoothly with black guipure lace as if
encrusted with it. Satin ribbon bows are very
effectively knotted on the front, and ends of
the ribbon are carried in pleats inside the belt.
The hat of fancy yellow straw is draped
around the brim with white appliqué lace, as
there is no canon at present against using two
or three different kinds of lace in one costume,

or indeed, upon the same gown. A cluster
of roses on the left side is held by loops of
yellow ribbon, while on the right are *choux*
of ribbon from which springs a ''Colonel''
aigrette. A parasol of light brocade has a fluffy
flounce of mousseline de soie with lace applied
on the edge, and a knot of ribbon on the
handle.

YACHTING COSTUME FROM WORTH
(7.7.1894, cover). The French yachtswoman's taste in dress differs greatly from that of her English sister. The latter wears a trim tailor-made gown of serviceable serge or linen, with a blouse and reefer of the simplest shape, and a sailor hat or yachting-cap like those worn by men. Something more fanciful both in stuffs and style is preferred by the Parisian. This gown is of white repped wool finely dotted all over the surface, a non-shrinkable stuff not heavier than serge, but far more effective. It is made with a Directoire basque of very simple shape, with revers of white moiré, and clasped by a moiré belt. The very full skirt is bordered with three bands of the wool, each edged with a narrow piping of white satin. A charming little collet to add when stiff breezes blow is of white wool of the gown. A Parisian touch is given in the thick waving puffs of white mousseline which trim the shoulders, and the full collar of mousseline around the neck. The Virot hat is of white straw wholly covered with white lace. Two *choux* of light green velvet are set under the brim. On each side of the crown are white and black birds with wings and tail pointed upward, as if preparing for flight. The low shoes are of white canvas, and loose large gloves of heavy white kid complete the attractive ensemble.

PARIS SPRING TOILETTE *(2.29.1896, p. 169).* Grayish-green silk in a large-branched broché design is the material of this costume. The skirt is of the prevailing godet shape. The front breadths are pleated in and the folds caught with a series of green velvet knots each held by a fancy button. A short Louis Seize coat has a full waved back and cut-away front opening widely on a double-breasted white silk vest with two rows of buttons. Very broad revers are faced with plain faille to match the brocade, and overlaid by the white revers of the vest. A large cravat of white chiffon drapes the bust. The hat of green straw is draped with a very wide ribbon, rising in loops at the back, against which rest black plumes.

SUMMER COSTUMES (6.16.1894, p. 476).
Fig. a: summer hat.
Fig. b: coiffure and collar trimming.

Fig. c: walking or travelling costume
Fig. d: riding-habit with vest.
Figs. e and f: bicycle costumes with divided

skirt.
Fig. g: sea-side dress
Fig. h: tennis gown.

A FRENCH AUTUMN CLOAK *(9.29.1894, cover).* The travelling cloak illustrated is of a lustrous cloth called drap de soie, which is rendered impermeable by a process that does not detract from its beauty. The carrick capes of the same and a large ruche of Tosca net around the neck make it rather ornamental. It is worn with a hat of dark rough straw or of stiff-brimmed felt trimmed with many loops of ribbon that form a large bow, and some clusters of flowers.

A GAME OF GOLF (*11.3.1894, cover*). Golf, our late British importation in the way of games, is becoming naturalized very fast. Since the establishment, some time ago, of the St. Andrews links at Yonkers, the oldest in this country, other places have steadily been falling into line. Newport, Tuxedo, Southampton, Morristown, Lenox, already have their clubs, and new links have just been laid at Orange and Montclair. At all these places women play the game, and they are admitted to membership in most of the clubs.

a   b   c   d

e　　　　　　*f*

WINTER AND SKATING COSTUMES *(12.1. 1894, p. 973)*.

Fig. a: fur-trimmed cloth costume.

Fig. b: velours du nord jacket.

Fig. c: coat for girl from 6 to 8 years old.

Fig. d: velveteen gown with Alaska sable.

Fig. e: Persian lamb jacket with Persian trimmed cloth skirt.

Fig. f: long plush coat.

LINGERIE *(2.15.1896, p. 132).*
Fig. a: sleeveless dressing sacque.
Fig. b: flannel morning jacket, back.
Fig. c: corset-waist for girl, 7 to 8 years old.
Fig. d: corset with shoulder braces for girl from 13 to 15 years old.
Fig. e: front of morning jacket.
Fig. f: corset cover and skirt.

LADIES' BLOOMERS AND COMBINATIONS *(11.13.1897, p. 952).* **Fig. g.**

TOILETTE FOR A BRIDE AND FOR THE MOTHER OF THE BRIDE *(2.29.1896, p. 168)*. **Fig. a:** toilette for mother of the bride. The gown is of Parma-violet faille. The skirt has on each side at the foot of the front a large *motif* of embroidery in silk and iridescent beads. A similar design is on the broad revers of the coat-bodice, which opens on a white satin vest draped by a jabot of deep point appliqué. Three-quarter puffed sleeves have flaring cuffs and drooping lace frills. **Fig. b:** bridal gown in princesse style with fichu.

PARIS SPRING WRAPS *(4.4.1896, p. 305).*
Fig. a: a smart little cape is of taffeta silk made with an empiècement of embroidered tulle, and finished with a ruffle of mousseline de soie. The collar is faced with a frill of white lace and has white lace tabs. A hat to wear with this cape is of fine straw trimmed with five ostrich plumes and bunches of yellow primroses. **Fig. b:** another fashionable cape is of stiff silk covered completely with embroidered tulle and trimmed with soft rosettes and a ruffle of mousseline de soie. The hat is inde-

scribably light and dainty; it is of straw, but covered over with tulle, in which are placed ostrich tips and bunches of roses. **Fig. c:** a wrap equally suitable for a young or middle-aged woman has a perfect-fitting empiècement of black net heavily embroidered in jet. From the empiècement starts a very full flounce of mousseline de soie edged with rows of narrow satin ribbon. The entire wrap is lined with stiff taffeta silk. The high collar is trimmed on the outside with bunches of mousseline de soie and inside with a white lace frill. The

hat shown with this wrap is of fancy straw, with bows of black and white lace, through which show glimpses of bright flowers. **Fig. d:** a cloth jacket fitted tight is quite distinctive with its revers faced with velvet and the sleeves buttoned to the elbow. The hat is in sailor shape, trimmed with accordion-pleated changeable taffeta. At the back are bunches of violets and roses with an aigrette formed of violets.

PARIS WALKING COSTUME FROM THE MAISON ROUFF *(4.25.1896, p. 365).* The skirt is trimmed around the bottom with five narrow folds of bias satin. The waist is cut into a short full coat, with broad revers, and the vest of taffeta the color of pigeon's breast, ornamented with fine embroidery in a Louis XV design. The front of the vest is softened by a full piece of Pompadour mousseline de soie. The belt and the cravat, which is tied in wing bows, are of the taffeta silk.

SPORTING COSTUMES *(5.30.1896, p. 464).*
Fig. a: gown with bolero jacket.
Fig. b: tailor costume for driving.
Fig. c: gymnasium suit.
Fig. d: shirt-waist and tweed skirt.
Fig. e: outing gown.
Fig. f: bathing suit.
Fig. g: mountain costume.

FRENCH PROMENADE COSTUME FROM THE MAISON WORTH *(7.11.1896, p. 588).* The material used in this gown is changeable moiré taffeta, the colors of a pigeon's throat. The skirt has box-pleated front while the back is in godets. The waist is trimmed most effectively with white mousseline de soie and a pleating of appliqué lace. A broad belt of white satin ribbon is finished at the side with a soft bow, while the collar matches the belt. The parasol is of chiné Pompadour taffeta trimmed with lace to match that on the waist of the gown, and the dainty hat of réséda straw is trimmed with flowers, a tuft of ostrich feathers, and a stiff lace aigrette.

PARIS CALLING COSTUME *(10.30.1897, cover).* Reception and visiting costumes this season are most elaborate in design and material. One very smart model from the Maison Revillon is of broadtail fur and moiré combined in an unusual and somewhat intricate design. With this gown is worn a collar of natural Russian sable made in Marie Antoinette shape. On the shoulders this collar is slashed, and two sable tails are put in, while all around the back of the collar are shorter tails. Around the neck is a high collar of chinchilla. A large Directoire muff is of the Russian sable, trimmed at the side with a bunch of five tails, and lined throughout with ordinary sable.

CASHMERE HOUSE GOWN *(10.30.1897, p. 904).* A gown that meets with general favor and is pecularly suitable for home wear has the waist made with a small, perfect-fitting yoke of black velvet, and high collar also of velvet. The blouse front, which hangs over the belt, is trimmed with crossed panels of black velvet ribbon, while the sleeves, which are made tight-fitting, have ruffles at the top and a pointed cuff at the wrist. On the skirt is the same pattern of black velvet ribbon, forming a regular design. The skirt is cut to train slightly, and is larger on the hips and in front than a walking skirt.

CLOTH GOWN WITH STITCHED SATIN BANDS *(11.13.1897, p. 947)*. Braiding of satin put on cloth is very greatly in favor this winter, and the more elaborate the pattern the better. A gown of dark blue smooth faced-cloth is noticeably smart, and the lines of the trimming are very cleverly designed. The skirt has bands of the satin going down the front and all around the foot, and the same pattern is carried out on the waist, the sleeves, and the square epaulettes over the top of the sleeves. An unusually deep rounded yoke is of tucked taffeta silk of shaded green. A high collar with inside frill of green is of the cloth like the skirt. On the waist and on the sides of the skirt below the belt are turquoise and rhinestone buttons.

CASHMERE GOWN WITH BLACK RUCHINGS *(11.13.1897, p. 947).* In the new shade of mignonette green is a cashmere gown trimmed with black ruchings of mousseline de soie with satin edge. The skirt is carefully fitted, and is not so sharply gored as usual, while the front breadth is wider. The waist blouses enough to be graceful, and fastens at the left side. The sleeves are nearly tight-fitting, with fulness at the top under double caps edged with the black ruching. The ruching trims the blouse around the yoke and square tabs at the left, and is also around the wrists and the foot of the skirt.

PARIS RECEPTION GOWN (*12.25.1897, cover*). An exceedingly effective gown is made with a skirt of velvet trimmed with a deep flounce of point-lace, which is appliquéd on to the velvet, and is bordered by a band of sable fur. The sleeves are of velvet, tight-fitting except just at the top, and made with deep cuffs edged with fur. The body of the waist is entirely of white lace, in blouse effect, made over a satin lining, with a high-stock collar, and flaring side pieces of velvet covered with lace. The distinctive part of the gown is a collar which is cut out in front and back like a square-neck dress, and this has a long stole end which broadens towards the foot of the skirt and hangs the entire length. The hat worn with this gown is a large soft velvet toque the same shade, trimmed with two long ostrich plumes fastened with a rhinestone buckle. Just under the brim to the left side is a rosette of satin ribbon with another rhinestone buckle.

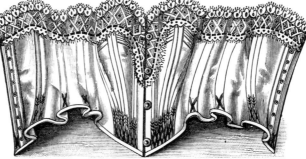

SUMMER COSTUMES AND LIN-GERIE *(7.9.1898, p. 592).*
Fig. a: young ladies' blouse-waists.
Fig. b: corset covers and combined corset cover and petticoat.
Fig. c: summer matinée of nainsook and lace.
Fig. d: linen shirt-waist costume.
Fig. e: lace-trimmed summer corset.

b   a

c

d

DEMI-SAISON GOWNS FROM PARIS
(8.20.1898, cover). **Fig. a:** checked tan gown. Every thorough summer outfit contains one or two thin woollen gowns that are worn early in the spring, on cool days in summer and then reappear in the autumn. A particularly smart one from Félix is of wood-color with a small check in the front and in the back, and is effectively trimmed with a yoke of fancy silk on which are lines of gold embroidery. Around the yoke and on the side of the waist that crosses over is a band of black velvet embroidered to match the yoke. Around the wrists are bands of the velvet embroidery, and just below the yoke in front the embroidery is put on to give the effect of a bow.

Worn with this gown is a hat from Virot, of yellow straw, and trimmed with ostrich plumes and a large rosette of black mousseline de soie. The brim has a narrow fold of black velvet inside, and is turned up at the left, showing a rosette of yellow mousseline de soie. **Fig. b:** blue serge gown. One of the newest models for a blue serge gown comes from Félix. In effect it looks somewhat like a redingote, but in reality is made with waist and skirt. The skirt, quite different from anything that has been introduced, is fastened at the side, and is elaborately trimmed with bands of black braid of different size, the lowest braid outlined with a fancy gold and red velvet on a bias band of white silk. The waist, fas-

tened at one side, has a most effective yoke of the fancy white silk embroidered in gold thread both in the front and back of the waist, and with a straight band collar with pointed pieces of the same silk. The sleeves are of medium size, with a puff at the top partly covered with a pointed epaulette, and are trimmed from shoulder to wrist with graduated bands of black braid; at the wrist is a line of the fancy gold braid. The hat worn with this gown is one of Virot's designs, and is of dark blue straw trimmed with black feathers and a large rosette of black mousseline de soie, with several deep red roses inside the brim at the left side. **Fig. c:** checked gown, back. **Fig. d:** blue serge gown, back.

PARIS MODEL FROM AUTUMN RECEPTION COSTUME *(9.17.1898, cover).* This most charming costume is of pale blue crêpe de Chine with black chenille polka dots, made in princesse effect. The waist is tight-fitting, although there is some fulness drawn in under the belt. It fastens on one side and shows a vest of white lace. On the skirt the same effect is repeated, the edge apparently lapping to one side, and showing beneath a deep flounce of lace. Around the vest and down the front of the waist and on the skirt are three rows of narrow black velvet ribbon, gathered quite full. At the throat is a double bow of mousseline de soie, and over the shoulders is worn one of the new style boas of white silk plissé, shirred into ruffles at regular intervals apart. Worn with this gown is a toque of blue tulle with black chenille dots and a black bird-of-paradise.

MOURNING ATTIRE *(8.27.1898, p. 728).*
Widows wear the deepest mourning that is
worn, and their veils are longer and the hem
deeper. Those who are very conventional as
regards mourning do not even have crape on
their gowns for some weeks; others again have
the entire gown made of crape, jacket and
skirt absolutely unrelieved. The first evening
gown that a woman wears when she goes out
into society after she has been in mourning
is generally of crape. Some most effective
dinner gowns have been made of crape heavily
trimmed with dull jet. All crape walking
gowns made with coat and skirt are also
trimmed with this dull jet. With such a gown
as this a bonnet without a veil is correct, and
it can be trimmed with the same style of dull
jet, however, not entirely of jet. After six
months of deep mourning, some women wear
white altogether in the house, trimmed with
black ribbons; all put white collars and cuffs
on black gowns—the very sheerest linen.

A PARIS TEA GOWN—MODEL FROM THE MAISON ROUFF *(10.10.1898, cover).* Among the newest importations for the autumn are tea gowns and house gowns (almost the same thing), that this year are more elaborate than ever, made of the most expensive coaterials, and trimmed with lace, ribbon, velvet, etc. A gown from la maison Rouff is especially noticeable, made of old-rose peau de soie, brocaded in blue and pink flowers. The waist is in a Figaro design, with appliqué of écru lace. A full double ruffle of mousseline de soie bound with black satin edges the jacket and extends around the neck, forming at the back a Medici ruff. There are two Figaro jackets, one put below the other, and the lower one trimmed with a smaller ruffle, which goes under the arms, and finishes at the back in the shape of a reversed V. The vest is of pink mousseline de soie plissé, shirred in at the waistline under the blue satin belt, and fastened at the side. Very full shirred sleeves are of pink mousseline, finished at the wrists with black edged ruffles. At the left side of the waist is a large blue satin bow with long ends that reach to the foot of the skirt. The skirt of the gown is long, and open in the front to show an apron of pink mousseline de soie. At the back the skirt hangs in three pleats to the foot, and there are deep folds at the side. In front the apron is trimmed with three spaced ruffles, and the brocade skirt at either side of the apron is edged with a ruffle.

❧ GLOSSARY ❧

Agrafe. A metal clasp or hook and eye, covered with braid, often jewelled, used as a decoration.

Aigrette. A cluster of upright feathers (originally plumes of an egret) or jewels simulating feathers.

Balayeuse. A dust ruffle basted on the underpart of a skirt to protect the hem from dirt. This ruffle could be removed and washed or discarded and replaced with a new one.

Bandeau (pl. Bandeaux). A narrow band worn either on the head or on the costume for decorative purposes.

Barathea. A closely woven fabric of silk and wool mixture.

Bashlik. A hooded shoulder cape with long ends, based on a Near Eastern outer garment. Popular during the 1860s.

Basque. A shaped, jacket-like bodice, fitting close to the body and often ending below the waist in a short peplum or skirt.

Bengaline. During the 1860s and 70s, a lightweight mohair with small floral patterns in self color. In later usage, a heavy-ribbed silk having a corded effect.

Bertha. A wide collar worn around a neckline, often made of lace, sometimes of matching or contrasting material.

Bouclé. A fabric woven or knitted to produce a knotted or curly surface.

Brandebourg (Brandenburg). A military type of braid trimming, sometimes in parallel bars, loops or frogs.

Bretelle. Suspender-like, shaped bands worn over shoulders and attached in back and front to a waistband. Often used to help support a skirt; sometimes applied as trimming.

Capote. A kind of head covering; a bonnet or a hood. Often a hat with stiff front brim and soft crown similar to a sunbonnet.

Carrick Cape. A mantle with one or more shoulder capes.

Casaque. A light coat-like garment worn outdoors.

Challie (Challis). A soft, lightweight fabric of wool or wool mixture, generally printed in a floral pattern.

Chemisette. A vestee or dickey, generally sleeveless and made of fine cotton and lace or net, used primarily to fill low necklines.

Chou (pl. Choux). A large, soft, cabbage-shaped rosette, made of fabric, lace or ribbons.

Corsage. Bodice or upper part of woman's dress. Also a draped fabric arranged over the ribcage portion of a waist. A bunch of flowers, real or artificial, used on a costume.

Crêpon. A fabric similar to crêpe, but heavier and firmer; generally of silk or a mixture.

Cretonne. A strong unglazed cotton fabric, generally printed in large floral patterns.

Cuirass. A jacket or bodice, lined and boned to fit smoothly over the torso. (Originally part of defensive armor for the upper portion of the body.)

Damassé. A damask-like fabric, usually having a reversible figured pattern.

Dolman. A wrap or cloak with cape-like, shaped sleeves which are wide at the shoulders and generally narrow at the wrists.

Duchesse. A highly lustrous satin, firmly woven but soft to the touch.

Écru. Natural unbleached color, generally beige or light tan.

Empiècement. A piece, such as a yoke, set in at the top of a garment.

Étamine. A light, loosely woven cotton or worsted fabric, often used for nuns' veils as well as for dresses.

Faille. A finely ribbed silk in a plain weave.

Fanchon. A cap or bonnet in the style of a kerchief folded on the diagonal to form a triangle.

Fichu. A small triangular or rectangular shawl or scarf, usually of fine soft fabric, worn over the shoulders and generally tied in the front like a kerchief.

Foulard. A fine soft silk or cotton in a twill weave, often printed in a small design.

Galloon. A narrow, tape-like trimming of rich material, such as lace with gold and silver.

Gamp. A large umbrella. (Named after Mrs. Gamp, a character in Charles Dickens's novel, *Martin Chuzzlewit.*)

Godet. A segment of cloth wider at the bottom. Used as an inset to produce fullness or for widening, such as in a skirt.

Grelot. Ball-fringe.

Grenadine. A fine, gauze-like fabric of silk or silk and wool, often printed but sometimes plain.

Gros Grain. A fabric or ribbon with heavy ribs woven horizontally.

Goutil. A lightweight cotton with a twill weave; sturdy and firm like ticking.

293

Guimpe. A waist-length blouse, generally of sheer cotton, with short or long sleeves and trimmed with lace or fine embroidery.

Guipure. A heavy lace with a large pattern.

Illusion Strings. Ties made of transparent silk tulle.

Jaconet. A thin muslin-like fabric.

Jardinière. A multicolored fabric having patterns of flowers, sometimes with fruit.

Jean. A strong, thick cotton cloth in a twill weave.

Lambrequin. A scarf worn over a hat as a protection against rain or heat.

Lampas. A damask-like fabric of silk or a silk mixture, with a double warp and one filling, generally colored.

Lisse. A smooth, fine gauze silk, often used for ruffles, ruches and trimmings.

Mantelet. A small cloak or short mantle, usually profusely trimmed with embroidery, ruffles, fringe or lace.

Matinée. A morning wrapper. A summer cloak, generally of cotton, worn over morning costumes.

Mechlin. A delicate bobbin lace made in Mechlin, Belgium.

Merino. A fine wool similar to cashmere.

Merveilleux. A silk or silk cotton mixture, woven in a twill weave with a lustrous finish.

Mignardise. A dress material, crocheted and having a design formed by narrow braid.

Mousseline de Soie. A gauze-like silk muslin.

Mozambique. A gauze-like fabric of silk and wool with a satin figure on the right side.

Mull. A very soft, fine, semi-transparent, lightweight cotton or silk in a plain weave.

Nankeen. A cotton cloth, generally of yellowish color.

Nansook. A thin, delicate cotton in a muslin weave.

Paletot. A cloak, usually loose, with one or more cape collars.

Panier. A structure or device worn at the sides to extend the hips. Also, a portion of a skirt arranged to provide fullness at the sides.

Parure. A matched set of ornaments, such as a necklace, earrings, brooch, etc.

Passementerie. Applied trimmings such as braid, cords and heavy embroideries.

Pelerine. A short shaped shoulder cape.

Pelisse. A full-length coat or cloak of silk, wool or cotton, often fur-trimmed, sometimes fur-lined.

Peplum. A short extension of a bodice or jacket flaring out below the waist over the hips.

Plastron. A V-shaped front of a woman's costume resembling the breastplate of a suit of armor.

Plissé. Fabric either chemically treated or resist-printed to produce puckers for a crinkled effect; generally arranged in a striped pattern.

Polonaise. A coat-gown with the fronts of the skirts pulled back over an underskirt.

Pongee. A lightweight, natural-colored textile, usually of silk with an irregular texture in a plain weave.

Poult de Soie. A rich corded silk. A fabric of silk and alpaca with a shiny surface.

Princesse. A gown shaped from shoulder to hem without breaking at the waist.

Redingote. A coat-dress worn over a skirt, sometimes of three-quarter length and buttoned down the front, often full-length and opened down the center of the front.

Revers (Reveres). The lapels on jackets, coats or dresses.

Ruche. A narrow band of net, lace, or fine, thin fabric, set in pleats or gathers. Applied to trim a dress, particularly at the neckline and wrists.

Sacque. An unfitted or semi-fitted bodice, jacket or robe.

Sicilienne. A mixture of silk and fine wool. A kind of poplin.

Sortie de Bal. An evening cape with a hood resembling a burnoose.

Surah. A soft twilled silk similar to foulard but heavier.

Tablier. An apron effect on a dress, popular from the late 1860s until the early 1880s.

Talma. A long circular cape, sometimes with a shoulder cape or hood.

Tarlatan. Thin, mesh-like, stiffened muslin.

Tilleul. Yellow-green, lime-colored.

Torsade. Trimming or an ornament simulating a cord or rope.

Toque. A round, close-fitting hat without a brim, usually somewhat squared off at the top.

Tournure. A bustle. A device or structure used to give the wearer's costume a hip extension.

Ulster. A long, loose-fitting overcoat worn by either sex for protection against the weather.

Vamp. Part of a shoe covering the toe and continuing around the instep.

Vandyke. An edging of long points similar to those on the collars and cuffs in paintings by Sir Anthony Van Dyck.

Vigogne. A neutral-colored wool in a twill weave.

Visite. A cloak, close-fitting in back, loose with extended ends in front.

Waist. The upper portion of a garment; the bodice. Another name for a blouse.

Watteau Back. A loose, flowing back with a set of box pleats sewn in back at the shoulders, then released to fall to the hem. Named after Antoine Watteau, the eighteenth-century French painter who portrayed ladies wearing unfitted sack-like gowns.

Yak Cloth. Fine wool mixed with yak hair in a twill weave.